STOP NOT TILL THE GOAL IS REACHED

Dr. Sanjeev Kumar Tiwari

PUSTAK MAHAL®

Publishers
Pustak Mahal®

Administrative office and sale centre
J-3/16 , Daryaganj, New Delhi-110002
☎ 23276539, 23272783, 23272784 • *Fax:* 011-23260518
E-mail: info@pustakmahal.com • *Website:* www.pustakmahal.com

Branches
Bengaluru: ☎ 080-22234025 • *Telefax:* 080-22240209
E-mail: pustak@airtelmail.in • pustak@sancharnet.in
Mumbai: ☎ 022-22010941, 022-22053387
E-mail: rapidex@bom5.vsnl.net.in
Patna: ☎ 0612-3294193 • *Telefax:* 0612-2302719
E-mail: rapidexptn@rediffmail.com

ISBN 978-81-223-1170-9

Edition: 2021

Printed at : Sharma Printers, Delhi

Contents

Preface

My quest for realisation of truth commenced just after my graduation. After completing my graduation in science, I had become disillusioned with life. I felt as if life had no meaning. Some fundamental questions of life suddenly started tormenting me and I desperately started seeking answers to those questions of life — Who am I? Why am I here on this earth? Where do I go from here? What is the purpose of human life? What is the goal of human life? What is death? Is there any life after death? Is death the end of everything or something remains after death? If death is the end of everything then what is the use of all these struggles? If there is God who is just and kind, then why there is so much pain and suffering in this world? Is there any meaning for our pain and suffering? What is the secret of life? What are the objectives of human existence? The acquisition of all means of comfort and luxury, having the best food and drink, and bringing up children and then dying a lonely death leaving everything – are these the only objectives of life? Is there nothing beyond this? What is the mystery behind life and death? Are there answers to all these questions?

One day I was going to Kolkata from Chinsurah by train to appear for some job interview. I was sitting by the window and thinking about those fundamental questions of life. Then and there, I found a hawker selling booklets containing quotations of Swami Vivekananda I bought a booklet for Rs. 2 and started reading the quotations. Finally I came to a particular quotation which enhanced the agitation of my mind. The quotation went like this – "The world is burning with misery. How can you sleep? … Arise, awake and stop not till the goal is reached". I became curious to know more about the quotation. I wanted to know what Swamiji had said before and after this particular quotation. What was the context in which it was said? I became desperate to gather further information. I felt that answers to all my queries regarding life can be found out by pursuing the background of this particular quotation.

At that very moment I completely forgot that I was going to appear for a job interview in Kolkata. In fact, instead of going to Howrah, I got down at Belur and went to Belur Math and bought all the volumes of 'The Complete works of Swami Vivekananda' available in the Math at that time. The next six months were spent in reading those books. In fact, in the next six months I did nothing except reading those volumes of Swami Vivekananda's work. After six months my life was changed. I felt as if I was enlightened. I got the answers to my all questions and felt inspired.

For the last one year I was groping in the dark and at last I felt as if Swamiji had held my hand and led me towards blessedness and immortality. His teaching had taught me the secrets of life sublime. By his blessings I was able to banish all my doubts, fears, sorrows and pain. At that moment I was reminded of one of the Swami Vivekananda's memorable sayings:

"So long as the millions live in hunger and ignorance, I hold every man a traitor who, having been educated at their expense, pays not the least heed to them. Those educated men who now wallow in comfort and luxury as a result of the sacrifice and hard work of millions of poor people who had been exploited have a duty to strive for the welfare of the poor people. If they don't do so, I call them traitors."

Immediately I felt I had to do something worthwhile in life. I made up my mind that henceforth, I would follow the teachings of Swamiji and become a teacher like him. I came to know from his biography that after his graduation he had taken admission in law. So, I felt I must also take admission in law. When taking admission in law I never thought of practicing law or becoming a judge or a law officer. I just wanted to become a teacher. My dream of becoming a teacher like Swami Vivekananda was fulfilled when I joined as a lecturer in a Government college after completing my LLM and I started preparing myself to meet the next challenge of life.

From the very first day of my joining the teaching profession I have been trying to inspire the students and everyone who came in my contact to realise their goal and missions in life. I have been trying to instill in them virtues which will make them good human being and enable them to achieve their goal and lead a fulfilling and happy life.

Now let me dwell a little bit on the reason behind writing this book. Actually, I feel I did not write this book on my own. Some divine power, my 'Baba' (I refer to God or the 'divine power' as my 'Baba'), compelled me to write this book. About ten months back, one fine morning, I felt quite restless but I did not know the reason for such restlessness. I prayed to my 'Baba' for guidance and peace. He communicated to me that I have certain mission to accomplish before my death and the mission is to communicate the truths which I have realised in my life so that it may act as a guide for the disillusioned people.

The moment I got this message from my 'Baba' all the restlessness of my mind vanished and I felt a strange kind of bliss and happiness. I had got my mission in life. 'Baba' wanted me to communicate to the world my realisations. That very moment I started putting into words my realisations – the truths and lessons I had learnt. I have chosen the written form to communicate my realisations to the world because I think written format is the best and most easily accessible way to reach the people. I have tried my best to narrate my experiences honestly without any exaggeration because I have always felt that truth alone has a lasting impression on people.

Throughout this book I felt as if 'Baba' was working through me. I felt as if I am just a medium of 'Baba', for laying down the fundamental truths of life. Often ideas and realisations came to me in a flash. Sometimes an incident in bus or train provided me with answers to some most complicated questions of life. Those lessons I used to jot down in my diary and that habit greatly helped me while writing this book.

I have full faith that this book will be able to solve most of your day-to-day problems if not all. If you minutely go through the pages of the book you will find the solutions to your problems in one or more of the pages of this book. Whatever your goal might be, this book will help you reach your goal.

This book will serve as a constant reminder that you cannot afford to stop till your goal is reached. The thoughts described in this book will act as an alarm clock to awaken you whenever slumber overpowers you. This book will act as your friend, philosopher and guide throughout your life. This book will also safeguard people and provide immunity against two deadly diseases of modern times – moral anaemia and spiritual cancer which have started spreading their deadly tentacles.

Start working today to reach your goal. Sometimes we keep on wishing without working. It is like just repeating the name of the medicine the doctor has prescribed for your illness loudly without actually swallowing it. You do not have to be a rocket scientist to know that just repeating the name of the medicine will not cure your illness. You have to swallow the medicine to do its work. If half the time people spend in wishing were spent in working, half of their wishes would soon be fulfilled and half of their dreams would come true. This book will help you in converting your wishes into actual realisation of your goals.

It is my humble request to readers to feel free to send me your feedbacks. It will greatly help in improving the book and making it more useful for them. I assure you that each and every letter from readers will be acknowledged with utmost love and care.

Dr. Sanjeev Kumar Tiwari
Phone – 9831012250
Email – SAMESIVUT@YAHOO.COM

Acknowledgements

At the very outset let me thank my 'Baba' for choosing me as his medium to write this book. As I have mentioned in the preface, this book could not have been completed without the divine assistance, blessings and love of my 'Baba', my God, regarding whom no question of believing arises, for I see and experience him every moment. Knock at his door, keep on knocking, and I tell you that if you are not discouraged, He will open it in due time and give all of a sudden what he has withheld for so long.

I wish to convey my gratitude to all the people involved in the writing of this book. I am thankful to all those authors from whose books I have drawn inspiration, such as Swami Vivekananda, Professor APJ Abdul Kalam, Shiv Khera, Barendra Kumar, Er M.K Gupta, Dayanand Verma, A.P Sharma, Dr. Devsare, A.P Periera, Carani.N. Rao, Walter Staples, Harry Lorayne, G.D Budhiraja, Norman Vincent Peale, Robert Schuller, John Mason, Mahatma Devesh Bhikshu, Swami Budhananda, Swami Jagadatmananda, Swami Ram Tirtha and others. It is not possible to mention the names of all the authors from whom I have got inspiration and knowledge, so even if your names do not appear here, let me assure you that I have valued your great help and am most grateful to you all.

I shall ever remain indebted to Swami Vivekananda, my spiritual guru, for his profound teachings, and especially for his life-transforming line *"Arise, awake and stop not till the goal is reached"*. As is evident, the title of this book is inspired by this famous quotation of Swami Vivekananda. I could not think of a better title than this to convey the message of my book. Moreover, when I was contemplating a suitable title for this book, all of a sudden the present title flashed in my dream and I was convinced about the suitability of the title.

I am very thankful to Mr. S.K. Roy of Pustak Mahal and his supporting team for their active cooperation at every step in bringing out this book in its present form. I remember the day when Mr. Roy told me over the phone that he liked the style of my writing and would be happy to publish the book.

My special thanks to all my teachers who have showered their blessings on me and shaped my career and made me competent to write a book of this nature.

My heart-felt thanks to my students who have always been at my side and are like my family. Let me take this opportunity to convey my love, blessings and best wishes to all my students wherever they may be.

My deepest gratitude to my grandmother, my parents, my brother and bhabhi, my wife, and my two sons for their unfailing emotional support during the writing of this book.

1

Small Incidents Change Life

Sometimes small incidents of life teach you so much which thousands of books would not have been able to teach. These small incidents sometimes affect or influence us so much that our life changes and we suddenly become a different person altogether. There are a lot of stories about great persons across the world which show how small-small incidents happened to their lives have changed their life or their attitude towards life.

Let me tell you the story of Tulsidas, the great Indian poet, who translated the 'Ramayana' into his language, Awadhi, retaining all the charm of the original work. The story goes back to the time when Tulsidas was a young man. He was married early to a beautiful lady, whose charm rendered him her slave. Tulsidas was passionately fond of his newly-wed wife. He could not live even for a moment without her. Once, she had to be away for a few days, but she was recalled soon after she left, because Tulsidas had fallen ill after her departure. Once, she happened to be at her parents' house without him. Tulsidas could not bear the separation and left for her parents' house.

By the time he reached the river bank it was pitch dark. Naturally, the boatman refused to ferry passengers across, even at four or five times the normal cost. He braved rough weather and swam across the swollen river late at night. As he struggled to keep afloat, something hit him – an object floating down the river. He clung on to it tightly and managed to cross the river, only to discover that it was a dead body.

When at last he reached her in-law's house, everyone was asleep. Ashamed of gate-crashing at that late hour, he scaled the wall of her wife's house, tugging at a python which he mistook for a rope. When his wife woke up and saw him blood-stained and shabby, she chided him for his blind infatuation for her and casually remarked that if only he had secured a fraction of such devotion to God, he would have secured his salvation. That was the signal for the spiritual awakening of Tulsidas who was at that instant transformed into a great devotee of God. He fell at the feet of his young wife and said, "You have shown me the way. You are not just my wife but my guru." He took leave of his wife, never to see her again.

Once Maharishi Dayanand Saraswati, the founder of Arya Samaj, was sitting on the bank of the holy river Ganga meditating quietly. He had chosen a lonely and quiet spot so that he would not be disturbed. However, his concentration was broken by the sound of sobbing. Distressed he opened his eyes to see a woman climbing down the steps to the river, carrying a small dead child in her arms. To his horror he saw the lady let go the dead child in the river. As she returned she collapsed on the steps of the river, weeping uncontrollably. Swami Dayanand Saraswati understood at once the poverty of the woman and the tragedy that had struck her. He saw and understood the misery and suffering of the poor and downtrodden. He decided then and there that he would take religion to the masses and serve them through religion.

Now, let me give one example from my own life.

As a teenager I was very undisciplined and disobedient towards my parents. I used to do whatever I thought was correct and would not pay any heed to the words of my parents. They would often try to correct me with advices and sermons but it was like playing music before a deaf person. All their attempts in correcting me failed and finally they gave up and allowed me to do as I liked.

One day, I was going by train to Kolkata. At Belur station a woman boarded the train and took the seat just opposite to mine. In her lap was a baby hardly 10-12 days old. I kept on looking at the baby and in a flash a thought arose in my mind that once upon I was also like this baby. How helpless it was! I was also helpless like this baby. How much love and care it would have required to make me what I am today. How much care and pain my mother would have taken to transform me from the tiny helpless baby to a full-grown man. How much pain I have given to my parents by being disobedient to them? Oh! What a sin I have committed by not listening to them? Tears rolled down my cheeks as I continued looking at the baby and remembering my mother. I did not feel like going to Kolkata. I wanted to return to my mother at home and cry in her laps for hours. I got down from the train and returned home. I had become a new person. What my parents could not teach me for years, that baby taught me in a few seconds. I felt as if a thick black veil of ignorance which covered my eyes had been lifted.

I went straight to my mother and said, "Mother forgive me for all the pains I have given you. Today I have realised the sacrifice of a mother. I will henceforth never be disobedient." It was a moment of bliss which cannot be described in words. It was one of the turning points of my life.

One day, Swami Vivekananda was returning from a temple when a troop of monkeys chased him. To save himself Swamiji at first started running, but the monkeys ran still faster and grew increasingly aggressive. At this time an old monk who happened to witness the scene called out to him – "Stop running. Face the brutes!" Swamiji heard his call and turned to face the monkeys. As soon as he faced the monkeys, they stopped harassing him and ran away.

Swamiji drew a great lesson from this apparently simple incident. He learnt that one should not run away when faced with danger or difficulty. Instead one must face it boldly In his later life, Swamiji referred to this incident while addressing a gathering in New York. He said:

"That is a lesson for all life – face the terrible, face it boldly. Like the monkeys the hardships of life fall back when we cease to flee before them. If we are ever to gain freedom, it must be by conquering nature, never by running away. Cowards never get victories. We have to face fear and troubles and ignorance if we expect them to flee before us."

This particular incident in the life of Swamiji and the lesson drawn from it had profound impact on me also. Whenever any problem comes in my life I remember this particular incident and I face the problem boldly and by the grace of God the problem is overcome quite easily.

Some of my students have the fear of speaking before the audience. They fear that they may become nervous in front of people and may get tongue-tied. I tell them that until and unless they stand before the audience and speak they can never overcome this problem. To overcome any problem you have to face it. The more you run away from the problem, the more the problem will chase you and haunt you. Maybe in your first attempt in speaking before the audience you may not be that good, but at least it will give you a lot of confidence when you appear again before the audience the next time. And gradually that fear will completely go away and you will become a good speaker.

In fact, I faced similar problem during my school days. I would always run away from debates, public speaking, etc., due to fear of facing the public. The result was that I never acquired the courage to stand in front of people and deliver a speech in my school days. It was only in the college that I learnt this valuable lesson from 'The complete works of Swami Vivekananda', that a problem can be overcome only by facing it boldly and not by running away from it. I started speaking in front of my parents first and then before my friends and then before my teachers and finally before general audience. I must admit that in the beginning I was not that impressive but gradually I gained confidence, and today I can confidently speak in front of delegates from different parts of the world in any seminar or conference.

Once a thief entered the hut of a saint named Pavhari Baba to rob him of his few belongings. As the thief was about to leave the place with the stolen goods, the saint woke up. This frightened the thief, and he threw down everything and started running away. Pavhari Baba promptly picked up the things and followed the thief. Finally, after a hot chase, he caught the thief and begged him to accept the goods. "All these are yours, my God," Baba told the thief, who stared at him in disbelief.

The thief was dumb-struck. Baba had addressed him as God and wanted to give him his belongings. He realised what a crime he had committed and how mean he was. From that moment he gave up his evil pursuit of material wealth and engaged himself in search for spiritual wealth. A few years later he got spiritual enlightenment and became a great saint.

During my college days I did not fully understand the value of time. I used to waste a lot of time doing unproductive things. I was not in the habit of planning things and following a daily routine. As a result, a lot of time got wasted in meaningless pursuits. Then one day, I read a book about Abraham Lincoln. I came to know that he was very punctual and people used to set their watches by following his daily activities. When Abraham Lincoln used to walk down the road, people corrected the time in their watches. People learnt about the exact time from Lincoln's walking time. If he had to arrive at any place at 10 a.m., he would reach that place on exact time, and people would know that since Lincoln has arrived so it is now 10 a.m. This quality of Lincoln changed my entire attitude towards time. I learnt the truth of the statement that "Time is wealth".

It will not be out of place to share another story with you all, which completely established in my mind the value of time and punctuality. The owner of London's famous jewellery shop, 'Masseurs Byron and Sons', used to close the shop at 4 p.m. sharp. He was very punctual. Opening and closing the shop at the right time was his passion. One day when he was closing his shop, a customer arrived to buy some jewellery.

Mr. Byron said, "I am sorry, the shop is closed. You may come tomorrow."

The customer said, "I am here to buy diamonds worth $ 4,00,000."

Mr. Byron said, "But the shop is closed, sir. Even if you buy all the diamonds in my shop, I will not open the shop. It is 4 p.m. now."

This story also had a deep impact on my mind and I realised the importance of punctuality. I always try to be punctual in all my visits, appointments, or meeting commitments. I learnt from these stories that the time we waste today will become our enemy tomorrow.

There was a student in my class who used to be very lazy and lethargic. Moreover, he used to waste lot of time in idle talks and doing useless things. He belonged to a rich family and used to wear fashionable clothes and branded watches. One day, I called him in my chamber and said: 'You wear branded and costly watches but you do not know the importance of time ticking inside those watches. The time ticking inside those costly watches are thousand times costlier than the watches themselves. So understand the importance of time or else it may be too late." These words had deep impact on him and from that day onwards he became a different person. He became disciplined in his activities and by proper utilisation of time he came out with flying colours in his exams.

Let me narrate an incident which opened my eyes and taught me a great lesson which perhaps no book would have been able to teach me. I had gone to visit one of my friends in Kolkata. In course of our conversation I told my friend that we had recently shifted to a new house in Chinsurah. My friend asked me the address of my new house. After giving the details of the address I said that it was orange coloured house and it would not be difficult to locate the house. My friend said that there may be other orange coloured houses in the locality, so how to know which one was yours. To close the matter I said that it was the biggest house in the locality. After few minutes my friend's seven-year-old son came up with a world map and said very innocently:

"Uncle you said your house is very big, so it can surely be located in this map. Uncle please show me your house in the map."

In that map Kolkata was shown by a dot and he wanted me to show him my house. His innocent question was very significant one. It made me realise the minuteness of our existence compared to the vast universe. Our ego makes us think of ourselves to be great and invincible but the reality is that it is nothing compared to the power of nature of God. I realised that ego is a balloon which may inflate or burst anytime, anywhere unexpectedly. Ego is an illusion which inspires to deceive at every step of life. An egoist is deep inside the well of mistakes.

That day, that innocent question of the boy had a great impact on me and it changed my attitude towards life in a positive way.

Once while going by train to my University, I was reading a book on Indian Penal Code. The gentleman sitting beside me started a conversation with me. Seeing me reading a law book and going by my young age he mistook me as LL.B student.

He was a police officer by profession and at once started lecturing me about different criminal laws. He also suggested me to study so and so books for getting good marks in LL.B examinations. One of the books suggested by him was 'Jurisprudence' by Dr. Sanjeev kumar Tiwari – yes the book written by me. How ridiculous! A person suggesting another person to read a book, written by the latter person. In his ignorance he praised me and my book. He also boasted about his wide knowledge in Indian Penal Code which was in fact very limited. Finally, when I was about to get down he asked me, "What is your name and in which year of LL.B you are studying?"

I said smilingly, "People call me Dr. Sanjeev Kumar Tiwari and I am a Professor of Law in Burdwan University." I did not wait to see the reaction on his face.

A few weeks later he came to my chamber in the University and apologised for his behaviour. He further said that he had learnt a great lesson that day and the lesson was that we should never underestimate others and overestimate ourselves. Just as he was parting he said that the day's incident had opened his eyes and dealt a severe blow to his egoistic nature.

We should never underestimate the intelligence or the talents of others, no matter how foolish they look or how silly their behaviour seems. We should remember that each one is unique in his or her own way, and God has created everyone with a unique purpose.

The following story drives home the above point in a humourous way:

A patient in the garden of a mental hospital sat holding a fishing rod over a flower-bed. A visitor approached, and wishing to amuse his companions asked aloud, "How many fish have you caught so far? "You are the ninth," the patient replied. The visitor was stumped by the answer of the patient.

Michael Faraday, the great scientist, was a simple soul. His simple clothes and modest behaviour often concealed from other his superior intelligence and genius. Once, a government official wished to meet Faraday. He went to the Royal Society where Faraday often worked, and asked to see the great scientist. He was directed to the lab where Faraday used to conduct his experiments. When the visitor entered the lab, he found it empty except for an old man in an overall, who was washing bottles in a sink.

"Excuse me, are you an employee of the Royal Society?" the visitor asked him.

"Yes, I have served the society for many years," said the old man. "What can I do for you?"

"Are you happy with the wages you get here?" the visitor persisted.

"I am content," smiled the old man.

"What's your name, by the way?"

"They call me Michael Faraday," came the reply.

The visitor was mortified. He had mistaken the great scientist for a security guard. How could a great man be so simple, he wondered. Or was he great because he was utterly simple? That small incident had taught the visitor the power of simplicity and he went home as a changed, but better person.

Gandhiji too, surprised people by his simplicity and humility. One day, Richard Cregg, an American admirer of Gandhiji arrived at the Sabarmati Ashram to meet the Mahatma. He was told that Gandhiji was in the common dining hall. Cregg wondered if Gandhiji was having his meal and whether he would disturb him by calling on him then. However, he found the dining hall practically deserted and entered inside only to find the great-soul, the leader sitting on the ground, peeling vegetables for the morning meal.

The American was overwhelmed by Gandhiji's utter simplicity. In a moment, he was sitting next to Gandhiji helping him with the vegetables.

Here I would like to share a story with you which I had read in a book. I tell this story to my students to inspire them to be courteous in their behaviour. The story goes like this—

At a grand banquet where American President Roosevelt and his wife were present, an old man approached Mrs. Roosevelt and greeted her respectfully. Mrs. Roosevelt returned the greeting graciously and spoke to him for some time. Emboldened by her courteous behaviour, the old man said to her, "Madam, may I bring my wife to you? She is always happy to think about the world of you and she will be delighted to have the opportunity to meet you in person!"

"May I ask you how old your wife is?" Mrs. Roosevelt inquired.

"She is about eighty-two Madam," the old man replied. "She is seated just outside this hall, in the anteroom. Shall I bring her here to meet you?"

"No sir," smiled Mrs. Roosevelt, "I should go and see her. You see, I am fifteen years younger to your wife and it is I who should go to see her not the other way round!"

This story epitomises courteous behaviour. A healthy society needs this kind of behaviour from every individual.

When Acharya Vinoba Bhave was still a kid, a stirring incident took place in his life. In their garden, his mother was tending to a papaya tree. It was not long before it bore the first fruit – a fairly large papaya. After obtaining permission from his mother, Vinobaji arranged to have the papaya plucked.

Excited Vinobaji then went to his mother so that he could lay his hands on the first piece! His mother told him to wash and skin it first. Thereafter, he was asked to cut it into fine pieces. Vinobaji could hold it no longer – the moment he had completed the task he rushed to his mother and sought permission to eat it.

It was then his mother asked him how many papaya trees were there in their village. Vinobaji said that theirs was the only tree and that was the first fruit the village had seen. So, his mother asked him then that how come the fruit from the tree was theirs alone. As it belonged to the whole village, Vinobaji was told by his mother to first offer it to all their neighbours and finally have his own share. And that is what he did.

He had learnt his lesson of sharing, understanding that everybody had a stake in the fruits of any effort as the entire society had directly or indirectly contributed to it.

Years later he said that this was the incident which laid the very foundation of the 'Bhoodan Movement' which was aimed at seeking the rich to hand over their excess land to the poor.

One day when I was giving lecture to my students in the class, suddenly the electricity went off. It was very hot and humid, and the students and myself too were sweating profusely. As I was totally engrossed in delivering the lecture I did neither realise that the fans were not moving nor feel any kind of discomfort.

Then a student stood up and said, "Sir, you are sweating profusely; we request you to take rest for a while."

I said, "Dear students, I love sweat because I believe sweat is the perfume of hard work. No perfume in the world can match the fragrance of sweat because other perfumes are made by crushing beautiful flowers but sweat is the result of your hard work and perseverance. So never dislike sweat, rather welcome sweat and love it."

Years later, when I was sitting in my chamber, a person came to me and touched my feet. As I blessed him he said, "Sir, I do not know whether you will be able to recognise me or not. I was your student and I passed out three years back. I am a Judicial Magistrate now."

I asked him how he was doing in life. He said, "Sir, I am indebted to you for all your lectures, but especially to the particular lecture where you had said, 'sweat is the perfume of hard work and you should love sweat'. That lecture made me throw away my lethargic attitude and made me a hard-working person. The lecture had changed my life. I think it is the result of that lecture that I am a Judicial Magistrate today."

**

2

Do It Now

Success comes to the man who does today what others think of doing tomorrow. You work and you win. You shirk and you lose. If you want to build and maintain a positive attitude get into the habit of living in the present and doing it now. You can leave footprints on the sands of time by making your life creative, cooperative and constructive; or you can leave the mark of heel by being destructive, despotic and desultory. Conditions are never just right. People who delay action until all factors are favourable do nothing.

The phrase *"do it now"* should be written on a piece of paper and must always be kept in the pocket. When you sleep keep the piece of paper under your pillow so that even in your dreams you are reminded of the phrase. Have faith in this phrase just as a Hindu has faith in the 'Bhagavad Gita', a Christian in the 'Bible' and a Muslim in the Holy 'Quran'. If you implement this phrase in your life, most of the problems of your life will be solved automatically. This phrase is like a life saving drug and if implemented it will work miracles in your life. This much I can definitely guarantee you.

The phrase *"do it now"* has changed my life in a positive way to a considerable extent. Many tasks which had been pending for a long time were completed within a short period by honestly and sincerely following this phrase. I could write two books on law in a period of one year by honestly following this phrase. I could write my poetry book in six months time, thanks to the magical powers of this phrase. I know many students who have achieved success and accomplished their goal by implementing this phrase in their lives.

James Alberry hits the right note in the following words:

"He slept beneath the moon,
He basked beneath the sun,
He lived a life of going to do,
And died with nothing done."

John Mason was quite correct when he said: "**The only thing necessary for the triumph of evil is for the good men to do nothing.**"

Time marches on. It tramples in its path the lazy, the idle, the wasteful, the unprepared and the inefficient. This does not mean that time is cruel. Time is just. It rewards the efficient worker. The persevering inventor rides on their crest of success. The enterprising businessman finds fortune, and the painstaking writer wins fame.

Let us listen to the views of **Shiv Khera** on the issue of procrastination. He says:

"Some people practice procrastination by hiding behind high-sounding words, saying I am analysing and six months later they are still analysing. What they don't realise is that they are suffering from a disease called Paralysis by Analysis and they will never succeed.

Then there is another breed of people who procrastinate by saying, I am getting ready. A month later they are still getting ready and six months later they are still getting ready. What they don't realise is they are suffering from a disease called 'executis'. They keep making excuses."

The most important time is 'now'. It is now or never. If you want to start any project or any new task just make the beginning at once because it might so happen that after some time you might lose that enthusiasm or you might be distracted by some other new problem and then it might so happen that your project would never see the light of the day.

When you put off until tomorrow certain task you will probably put off tomorrow too. Successful people are those who get up from their seat and take immediate action. The right time for starting or doing an appropriate thing is 'just now' and not 'tomorrow'.

Vivian Laramore puts it beautifully:

**"I have shut the door on yesterday
And thrown the key away,
Tomorrow holds no fears for me,
Since I have found today."**

Procrastination is not only the thief of time, it is the thief of progress, accomplishment, achievement, and duty. It turns all life's missions and goal to nothing. Avoid the habit of procrastination or postponement. Do not give in to indulgence and ease. When you fail to attend to your duty, you will continue to feel restless, disturbed and tensed. Relaxation and ease only come to you with the successful completion of your allotted duties. The procrastinators are good at talking, not doing. They will make all the plans but never start the journey. They intend to make a palace but they are never able to build a hut. They will just talk and talk but do nothing. Therefore, devote your full attention and concentration to the task at hand. Do not make half-hearted attempts at anything you do because half hearted attempts do not produce half results, rather it produces no result.

Benjamin Franklin was not incorrect when he said:

"Never leave till tomorrow, which you can do today."

No person has ever been able to do anything tomorrow. Whatever great things have happened in the world, they were done only by those persons who had always emphasised 'today' and not 'tomorrow'. Only talking and lingering things day by day is a sure sign of heading towards failure. Avoid laziness and take action 'here and now' and not in some imaginary future.

Shiv Khera presents a beautiful example of procrastination. He says, **"This is like the little boy who says when he becomes a big boy, he will do this and that and will be happy. And when he becomes a big boy he says that when he finishes college he**

will be happy. And when he finishes college he says when he gets his first job he will be happy. And when he gets his first job he says that when he gets married, then he will be happy. And when he gets married he says when the kids get out of school he will be happy. And when the kids get out of school, he says that when he retires, he will be happy. And when he retires, what does he see? He sees life has just gone by in front of his eyes."

Some days back a student came to me to consult regarding an essay competition in which he wanted to participate. After giving him the necessary guidance I asked him to go home and start writing the essay at once. Unfortunately he did not pay heed to my advice and made up his mind to start the work tomorrow morning. In the morning when he was about to start the work of essay writing, his maternal aunt came from her native place to his house. He got busy with the necessary formalities and could not begin the work that day. At night he promised himself to begin the work next day early in the morning. In the morning he became ill and was bed-ridden the entire day. After two or three days when he became healthy, he had lost the enthusiasm and the motivation to participate in the essay competition. Thus he became the victim of procrastination and lost an opportunity to show his talent.

The hours you lose today are gone forever. You will get another twenty-four hours tomorrow, but you cannot recall single hour of yesterday. What you lose, you cannot reclaim. So too with life – once lived, it is over and done with. You may regret it, you may be proud of it, but you cannot live it over again.

John Mason puts the thing quite effectively when he says:

"Most people who sit around waiting for their ship to come in often find it is 'hardship'. The hardest work in the world is that which should have been done yesterday. Hard work is usually an accumulation of easy things that should have been done last week."

The secret of getting ahead is getting started. Once you get going, the going gets easier. A journey of thousand miles begins with first step. Never put off for tomorrow what must be done today. Grasp every opportunity to help the depressed and encourage the young and inexperienced by being quicker to praise than to blame. We wear branded watches but do not know the importance of time ticking inside the same. It has been rightly said that killing time is not murder, it is suicide. Procrastination is the grave in which opportunity is buried. Two things rob people of their peace of mind – work unfinished and work not yet begun.

It has been rightly said by **A.P Pereira**–

"Be prompt in the execution of your work. Don't leave for tomorrow what you can do or finish today. Above all, be slow to promise but quick to perform. A hazard left untouched grows in size by the hour. An obstacle which can be removed easily today, may become too big for you tomorrow".

According to **Balthasar Gracian,**

"**The wise man does at once what the fool does finally**."

Take care of today and tomorrow will be easier to take care of. Take care of this week and this month will give you little trouble. Take care of this month and the year is sure to be a success. Take care of today. There is no better way to take care of the future. Think about the best things in the morning. Plan your day ahead and then work out your plans. It is a good habit to plan your day in advance. A proper planning saves lot of your time.

Tackle any difficulty now – the longer you wait, the bigger it grows. The first step to overcoming procrastination is to eliminate all excuses for not taking action. When you won't start, your difficulties won't stop. It is surprising how once a work is started the difficulties of a task tend to vanish.

It has been rightly said by **Barendra Kumar**, the author of the book 'Can is the word of power'—

"All the treasures on earth cannot bring back a single lost second, a single lost minute. Life is precious. So also is time. It

cannot be purchased, borrowed, hoarded. It can only be spent, invested – wisely or unwisely. So why to waste something you can't recapture. Be careful about your time. You will suffer, if you lose it; you will repent, if you abuse it. You will feel happy, feel better, feel great, if you use it. Use it now."

Tomorrow is such a disappointing day. It always promises to be a day we have been waiting for, hoping for, expecting for years and years. Alas! It proves to be just another day. And we will make no more use of it than we have made of today. When you say you will do the thing someday, it means 'no day' because 'someday' is not any day of the week.

I had read a poem in a book of **A.P Pereira** which beautifully depicts the truth regarding procrastination. The poem goes like this—

"Every day that comes and goes,
Every mile the river flows,
Says to me and says to you:
Much there is to learn and do,
And the water and the day,
Never more will pass this way."

Sometimes we find people not doing anything but still appearing to be successful. We feel that the divine law or the law of 'cause and effect' is being violated. We feel the futility of working hard in such situations. We feel cheated and depressed. In such a situation **John Mason** comes to our rescue.

Just listen to **John Mason** on this point. He says:

"Occasionally, you may see someone who does not do anything appearing to be successful in life. Do not be deceived. Remember the old saying – Even a broken clock is right twice a day."

Success doesn't come from outside. It is in your brain. As soon as you think a right thought, work it. Some people have a good idea but they haven't the tenacity to think it through and work it out. You must have courage and perseverance, and think

"I am going to see my idea through. It may be that I won't win out in this life, but I will make the effort." Every idea is a little seed, but you have to grow it.

According to **John Ruskin**,

"The whole youth period is to be used for learning and increasing knowledge. There is not a single moment of life that is inept for building fate. If you do not avail the chance to learn and time also passes, it shall never come back. If the hot iron piece becomes cold, there is no use beating it with a hammer, for it would not be transformed into a shape desired by you."

***

3

Let Bygones Be Bygones

Let me start this chapter with the words of **Thomas Jefferson.** He said:

"I like the dreams of future better than the history of the past."

You can't have a better tomorrow if you are thinking about yesterday all the time. As **John Mason** says: **"Never let yesterday use up too much of today."**

Everybody knows that it is useless to cry over spilt milk. But we keep on forgetting this wonderful proverb and continue crying as if with crying the milk will automatically come into the container once again, and will be pure and tasty as before. Every day is a new day. Every day a new beginning can be made. Every day new challenges can be undertaken. Every day new resolutions can be made. If you have committed mistakes in the past it does not mean that those mistakes cannot be remedied. If you have made wrong moves in the past it does not mean that it cannot be corrected. The problem will be solved when you realise that happiness is a present attitude and not a future condition.

Suppose a room is full of darkness and you come in and begin to weep and wail, "Oh it is so dark." Will the darkness go away? If you keep on crying the darkness will not vanish. On the contrary it will create more darkness. What you have to do is to bring a candle and light it and in a moment the darkness will vanish.

G. D Budhiraja writes:

"One of the most tragic things I know about human nature is that all of us tend to put off living. We are all dreaming of

some magical rose garden over the horizon, instead of enjoying the roses that are blooming outside our windows today."

A saint is just a sinner who fell down and got up. Your past should be a reference point, not a residence. You have to realise that what happened yesterday is gone. You can never get that time back and, therefore there is nothing you can do about it. But right in front of you is another minute or another hour or another day, week, month, year. Those things haven't happened yet, so you can start to orchestrate your present so that your future will be more to your liking.

Let us look at the profound thought of Roman poet **Horace**. He writes:

"Only that man is happy
Who can claim 'today' as his own
Who unconcernedly says safely,
Happily and fearlessly—
'I have lived today
You may do whatever tomorrow.'

Remember your past cannot be changed, but you can change your tomorrow by your actions today. Forgetting the past is absolutely necessary for a successful future. Past should be used only for learning some lessons from it so that these mistakes are not repeated. Besides this, there is no importance of past.

Let us remember what **Robert Louis Stevenson** said:

"Anyone can carry his burden, however hard, until nightfall. Anyone can do his work, however hard for one day. Anyone can live sweetly, patiently, lovingly, purely, till the sun goes down. And this is all that life really means."

You may have noticed that children are never depressed. They are always active, cheerful and full of enthusiasm. One reason that children are so noticeably happy and have seemingly impossible energy is that they have very little past to bog them down. Children do not think about the past. They always live in the present and therefore, enjoy life the most.

Charles F. Kettering once said:

"I am not interested in the past. I am only interested in the future, for that is where I expect to spend the rest of my life."

Present moment is the most important moment of your life. What matters most to you and to the world right now is what you are at present and not what you were or will be.

Every night when you lie down to sleep, practice dropping all failures and mistakes into the past. They are over, finished. Look confidently to the future. God gives you new opportunities every morning.

Norman Vincent Peale says:

"Every day is a new beginning so is every new month. Perhaps that is why God brings down the curtain of night – to blot out the day that is gone. All of your yesterdays ended last night. It makes no difference how long you have been alive, they are all ended. This day is absolutely new. You have never lived it before. What an opportunity?"

John Mason puts the things in right perspective by remarking—

"Rosy thoughts about the future can't exist when your mind is full of the blues about the past."

Once a student of law came to me with some personal problems. He said that he was depressed because he had messed up his life. He said that he had been taking drugs for a long time and he believed that he has reached a point of no return. I told him to burn all his past just now in the imaginary fire in his mind and throw the ashes into the imaginary sea in his mind. I told him to start a new life from this very moment with no past. Think as if you have taken birth in this world just now. I also told him to use his past as a spring board and not a hammock. I further told him not to make his past become memorials. Rather the past should be cremated and forgotten. He took my advice seriously and started his life afresh. He was not only able to quit the drug altogether but also became a very successful lawyer after some years.

Oscar wilde was straight on the mark when he said: **"No man is rich enough to buy back his past."**

Hubert Humphrey gives us a wonderful thought—

"The good old days were never that good, believe me. The good new days are today, and better days are coming tomorrow. Our greatest songs are still unsung."

Just mark the words of **G.D Budhiraja**. He says: **"Just because you made a mistake or circumstances led you to do something that you now regret, does not mean that for the rest of your life you will have to beat yourself up because of it. Doesn't matter if you made two mistakes or three. It does not even matter if you made over a million mistakes in your life. What matters is today, right now."**

Every day in the morning, the rising sun brings with it a new hope and new opportunities. Every day a new beginning can be made for a better life. This very moment everything about the past can be set aside and new life can be started with firm resolve and determination. Throw away all your weaknesses and challenge life with your will power and determination and see how life falls at your feet and surrenders to you. Stand tall and face the challenges of life. Forget the illusion called 'past'. You are not married to it. Don't have the misconception that you have an obligation towards the past.

Edna Ferber says:

"Living in the past is a dull and lonely business. Looking back strains the neck muscles, causing you to bump into people not going your way."

It has been rightly said by **Philip Raskin**: **"The man who wastes today lamenting yesterday will waste tomorrow lamenting today."**

Our main business is not to see what lies dimly at a distance, but to do what is clearly at hand. We should not be excessively preoccupied with the events of tomorrow. Rather we should set ourselves in sphere of action today. It should be remembered that dreams of future are more valuable than the history of the past.

John Mason gives us a valuable advice. He says: **"Use the past as a launching pad and not a lawn chair."**

If your past is full of thorns it will not be a wise thing to make a pillow of those thorns and put your head on it. It will give you pain rather than comfort. Of course if your past is full of roses, you can surely make a pillow of those roses and have a sound sleep. Do not take pride in becoming the tragic hero by brooding over your sorrowful past and slowly but surely destroying yourself. Believe me there is no fun in this and for this act of yours no statue will be erected in your memory.

**

4

Have Courage to Take Risks in Life

I like to start this chapter with the words of **Dorothy Carnegie**:

"Take a chance. All life is a chance. The man who goes furthest is generally the one who is willing to do and dare."

One of the greatest tragedies of life is that, people always try to play safe. They do not think how to win but are concerned how not to lose. The result is that we become satisfied with the 'good' and do not strive to reach the 'best'. That is why it is said that 'good' is the greatest enemy of 'best'.

People who do not take any risks remain the same throughout their lives. To fully manifest your talents and potentialities you have to take risks in life. A person who wants to become a pilot has to get into the cockpit and fly in the sky. You cannot become pilot by crawling on the four on the floor of your dining room.

Herbert Casson points out—

"Safety first has been the motto of human race but it has never been the motto of leaders. A leader must face danger. He must take the risk and the blame and the brunt of the storm."

If you never take risks you will never accomplish great things. A dream that does not include risk is not truly worthy of being called a dream. Too many people expect little, ask for little, receive little, and are content with little.

Babul Supriyo, the famous playback singer, was three years senior to me in Don Bosco Bandel. After completing his studies he got a secure job with handsome salary. He could have continued with his job and reached top level in that job but his passion was in singing. One day he resigned his secured job and moved to Mumbai. Everybody hailed his decision as foolish one but Babul Supriyo was bold enough to take the risk and had faith in himself. He struggled for some time but soon tasted success and today Babul Supriyo is famous and popular not only in India but abroad also. How many of us would have left such a secure job and tried our luck in a profession where there is so much struggle, competition and uncertainty. But Babul Supriyo believed in the maxim, "Until you enter the beehive you cannot take the honey."

Listen to what **John Mason** says:

"Whenever you see a successful person I guarantee he or she took risks and made courageous decisions. Success favours the bold. If you have found yourself throughout life never scared, embarrassed, disappointed or hurt, it means you have never taken any chances."

If your life is ever going to get better you will have to take risks. There is simply no way you can grow without taking chances. If you are afraid of getting burned, better stay out of the kitchen. If you are going to fight for principles and convictions, you can hardly avoid a rough time now and then. If you do not dare you will not get your share and will never become rare.

William the conqueror decided to back himself into a corner when he successfully invaded England. He burned his boats on the beaches as soon as he landed, leaving his armies no escape. Then he had to win, and he didn't have time to think of a way out if he lost – there was no way out. We should always remember that we were forced out of the comfort zone of the womb by nature but we must break out of the comfort zone we have created in our life all by ourselves.

That life is full of risk and it is difficult to avoid risk is evident from this beautiful poem.

To laugh is to risk appearing fool,
To weep is to risk appearing sentimental,
To reach out for another is to risk involvement,
To expose feelings is to risk exposing your true self,
To love is to risk not being loved in return,
To live is to risk dying,
To hope is to risk despair.
To try is to risk failure,
But risks must be taken, because the greatest
Hazard in life is to risk nothing,
The person who risks nothing, does nothing,
Has nothing and is nothing.
They may avoid suffering and sorrow, but they
Cannot learn, feel change, grow, love or live
Chained by their attitudes, they are slaves,
They have forfeited their freedom.
Only a person who risks is free.

If you dare for nothing you should hope for nothing. If you do not risk anything you risk even more. I strongly believe in the saying: "The greatest risk of life is not taking any risk." It is better to be a lion for a day than to remain sheep all your life. If we yield to temptation, life may be easier but it certainly will be less interesting.

Robert Schuller was absolutely correct when he said: **"The people who are really failures are the people who set their standards so low, keep the bar at such a safe level, that they never run the risk of failure."**

Let me tell you the story of one of my students named Rajib Bhattacharya. Rajib had completed his Masters in Law and was looking forward to a career in legal profession. But unfortunately he got a job of schoolmaster through West Bengal School Service Commission. It was a secured government job with good salary and it tempted Rajib to join the service. I have said Rajib's getting of a secured government job as 'unfortunate' because it limited his potentialities and talents. Since he became satisfied with 'good' he was prevented from reaching the 'best'.

After about one year he met me and I asked him how he was doing? He said that he was not getting job satisfaction and felt depressed. I asked him whether he wanted to remain a schoolmaster all his life or he wanted to become a judge of High Court? He said of course he wanted to become a judge. Then I asked him whether he had enough courage to tender his resignation from the present job as schoolmaster? He told me that he needed to consult his parents and well-wishers. Everybody told him that it would be foolish decision to take such a big risk. But fortunately Rajib listened to my advice and resigned from his job. After that he seriously started preparing for judicial service and after six months he cleared the Tripura Judicial Service and now is posted in Agartala as Judicial Magistrate. I am sure one day he will accomplish his dream of becoming a High Court judge.

Alexander Graham Bell said:

"Don't forever keep on the public road, going only where others have gone. Leave the beaten path occasionally and dive into the woods. You will be certain to find something you have never seen before. One discovery will lead to another."

If you have a choice of taking two paths, always take the more daring of the two. Calculated risk often produces extraordinary results. There is no substitute for courage and though the chance of hurting your toe increases the more you walk, it is always better than going nowhere by standing still. Take chances, take smart risks and you will meet with success beyond your dreams.

W.J. Slim said:

"When you cannot make up your mind which of the two evenly balanced courses of action you should take – choose the bolder."

There is a thought-provoking story given by **Shiv Khera** in his book 'You Can Win'. It goes like this. Once someone asked a farmer if he had planted wheat for the season. The farmer replied, "No I was afraid it wouldn't rain." The man asked,

"Did you plant corn?" The farmer said, "No I was afraid that insects would eat the corn." Then the man asked, "What did you plant?" The farmer said, "Nothing. I played it safe." This is the story with most of us. We play it safe and in the process we waste our talents and fail to make maximum use of our lives.

So **Shiv Khera** said correctly,

"All positive changes require sacrifice and discipline. The path is full of risks and obstacles. Our patience and resolve will be put to test. There shall be threats, criticism and condemnation. The greatest danger of all, however, would be to do nothing."

It is difficult not to get inspired by the following words of **George Bernard Shaw—**

"People are always blaming their circumstances for what they are. I don't believe in circumstances. The people who get on in this world are the people who get up and look for the circumstances they want, and if they can't find them, make them."

Your willingness to risk is the only real measure of your desire to be successful but analyse and minimise risk in the pursuit of success. Courage means willingness to take risks, to accept challenges. Nothing positive happens until you take full responsibility for your thoughts and actions. Successful people take responsibilities for their own lives, where as unsuccessful people duck responsibilities.

According to **Carani N Rao,**

"Most failures are not due to lack of luck but due to lack of pluck."

Let me tell you the story of two seedlings which in a very simple way highlights the consequence of not taking any risk in life.

One day two seedlings fell on the earth and they got covered themselves with soil. They slept happily in the night. They got up in the morning. One said, "Wake up. It's morning time." The other seedling replied, "So what? The sun has to rise yet. Let me sleep." The first one said, "You keep on sleeping. I am going out of the ground." The other tried to stop him and said, "It's dangerous to come out of the ground. People will harm you and kill you." The first one did not listen to his advice and emerged out of the ground. Thus it felt happy to see the beauty of the world. The sun showered its light on it. Pleasant breeze tickled it and it quenched his thirst through rain. This seed started growing and turned into a beautiful tree bearing lot of beautiful flowers. When it died it left infinite seedlings behind, with a feeling of satisfaction that it had perpetuated life. On the other hand, the other seedling afraid of taking risk, remained inside the earth and could not enjoy the joy and happiness of the outside world as enjoyed by the other one.

Harry Truman once said:

"If you are afraid of getting burned, better stay out of the kitchen."

If you attempt little, you will accomplish little. If you attempt big, you will accomplish big. It is as simple as that. If you are playing it safe you are creating more insecurity for yourself. Go and jump in the battlefield of life. It is better to die on the battlefield than to live a life of coward. Progress always involves risk. If you want to develop, progress and scale new heights you have to take risks. A soldier riding a horseback can fall and die but a worm crawling on the floor can never fall because the worm plays it safe. But there is glory in the living and also in the death of the soldier but in case of a worm there is neither any glory in its living nor in its death. Now, you have to decide whether you want to become a soldier or a worm.

Courage is the quality to act, as you believe. Courage gives conviction to act, to do what you feel, to be right. Courage gives moral strength and helps you to start as you think and believe, thus moves you to fulfil your goal.

It has been rightly said by **Winston Churchill**—

"Courage is rightly esteemed the first of human qualities because as has been said, it is the quality which guarantees all others."

Live as brave men with brave hearts. Live as lions and die like a lion. It is better to live like a lion for a single day than to live hundred years like worms. Take the bullets of life on your chest, not on your back. Courage is life, cowardice is death. Who says you cannot make a hole in the sky. Just throw a stone at the sky with great enthusiasm and courage and see how the stone pierces the heart of the sky.

William Shakespeare said:

"Our doubts are traitors, and make us lose the good we often might win by fearing to attempt."

One, who has strong desire to succeed, becomes great. Those, who have no desire to succeed or excel, can't do anything in life. They simply fail and regret. They do not trust their abilities and give up before commencing a task. All scientists, researchers or courageous people have strong desire to succeed. Their desire provides them with enough energy to gain victory.

I was really inspired by the words of **Seneca – "It is not because things are difficult that we do not dare; it is because we do not dare that things are difficult."**

Theodore Roosevelt's following words still echo in our ears and inspire us:

"It is not the critic who counts; nor the man who points out how the strong stumbled or where the doer of the deed could have done better. The credit belongs to the man who is actually in the arena; whose face is marred by dust and sweat and blood; who strives valiantly; who errs and comes up short, again and again; who knows the great enthusiasm, the great devotion, and spends himself in a worthy cause; who at the best knows in the end the triumphs of high achievement, and who at the worst, if fails, at least fails while daring greatly; so that his place shall never be with those cold and timid souls who know neither victory nor defeat."

There is so much truth in the following words of **Vincent Van Gogh**:

"What would life be, if we had no courage to attempt anything?"

It has been rightly said by **Shiv Khera** that life is not a spectator sport. Onlookers criticise, but they don't want to get involved. They are free-loaders. They want anything and everything for free. They do not want to pay a price; they do not want to earn anything. They should either get involved or shut up.

❊❊

5

Always Have Positive Attitude

Let me start this chapter with the beautiful words of **James Allen**. He said:

"All that a man achieves is the direct result of his own thoughts. A man can only rise, conquer and achieve by lifting up his thoughts. He can only remain weak and abject and miserable by refusing to lift up his thoughts."

A study conducted in Harvard University found out that when a person gets a job or a promotion, 85% of the success is because of his attitude, and only 15% of it is because of his intelligence and knowledge of specific facts and figures. It is surprising that we spend so much in learning facts and figures which account for only 15 % of success in life.

The following story, told by **A.P Pereira** will put more light on the findings of the above study. The story goes like this—

A merchant needed a clerk. He placed an advertisement in a newspaper and applications were received. Twelve of the applicants were called for selection. The merchant called them in his room one by one and finally selected one of them.

A friend of the merchant, who was in the room, was surprised to see that the boy who was selected was not a highly educated as some of the others who had been sent away.

"Why did you select this one?" he asked the merchant. "He has not passed the high school examination and has no other claims to the job."

"You are correct when you say that the boy is not highly educated," answered the merchant, "but you are wrong when you say that he has no other claim to the job. In fact, he has great many."

"First when he entered the room," continued the merchant, "he closed the door gently after him. This shows that he is careful and considerate of the feelings of others."

"Second he picked up a book that was lying on the floor and placed it on the table."

"Third his hair was well combed and his clothes, though old, were neat and tidy. What better claims than these can a boy have to a job?"

These are trifles, you may feel. Of course they are trifles — but they are tremendous trifles, and they make all the difference between success and failure, employment and unemployment, happiness and frustration.

According to **William James,**

"The greatest discovery of my generation is that human beings can alter their lives by altering their attitudes of mind."

Attitudes are more important than facts. And there is no doubt at all that if you consciously look for the best in things instead of the worst, it will act as a tonic for your mind and heart, tending to remove the tensions that stifle the creative unconscious. A positive attitude will make you grow. You will be able to achieve happiness and spread it around, making the world a better place. Positive attitude can be a stepping stone to success whereas negative attitude can be a stumbling block. A person with positive attitude is like a fruit of all season. He is always welcome everywhere. Positive orientation can actually keep life worth living and can possibly extend your life period.

No one can insult or hurt you without your permission. One of the golden keys to happiness and great success is the way you interpret events which unfold before you. Highly successful people are master interpreters. People who have attained greatness have an ability which they developed to interpret negative or disempowering events as positive challenges, which will assist them in growing and moving even farther up the ladder of success. There are no negative experiences, only positive experiences which aid in your development and toughen your character so that you may soar to new heights. There are no failures, only lessons.

Martin Luther King Jr has rightly said:

"If a man is called to be a street sweeper, he should sweep streets just as Michelangelo painted, or Bethoven composed music or Shakespeare wrote Poetry. He should sweep streets so well that all the gods of heaven will pause and say, here lived a great street sweeper who did his job well."

Small differences in your personal repertoire of knowledge can lead to major differences in your income and achievements. Small differences in ability can lead to enormous differences in results. The winning horse in the race wins 10:1. Is it 10 times faster than the other horses? Of course not. It may be faster by a fraction of second or by a nose, but the rewards are 10 times greater. The same is true in our lives. Successful people are not 10 times smarter than the people who fail. They may be better by a nose, but rewards are ten times bigger.

Thus striving for excellence is progress, because there is nothing that cannot be done better or improved. All we need is a little edge. Always strive for excellence, not for perfection because if you always look for perfection you will be disappointed with yourself if the work is not perfect. Perfection is not in our control but excellence is within our power and reach. Excellence means giving your best and working to your full potential. It may not amount to perfection but there will be satisfaction of giving your best under the circumstances. Moreover, consistently striving for excellence may one day bring perfection also. So do not settle for mediocrity, but always strive for excellence.

Once while visiting a fair I had met a person who had literally no face. There were no eyes, no nose, no mouth was visible apart from a small hole, no ears, no eye-brows. There were just two holes which acted as his nostrils. He had deformities in his hands and legs also. He was seen roaming in the fair begging. I was stunned by the will-power of the person and his love for life. Any other person would have contemplated committing suicide. But this person had the determination to fight it out despite these serious limitations. I was inspired by his jest and enthusiasm for life. We get panic and become almost mad when a small boil appears on our face and here was a man living without a so called face and still appearing so enthusiastic and lively.

Now, whenever any trouble arises I think of that person and in a flash my worries are tossed over the sea. I feel my troubles and worries are nothing in comparison to that person and thinking of that person makes me forget my sorrows because it appears so small and insignificant in comparison to the pain of that person.

Seeds look so small, yet in a tiny seed may have the potential of a huge tree, with towering trunk and heavy branches. But the potential alone doesn't make the tree. You have to put the seed inside the ground, give it water and look after it. Then, when the tree is full-grown, you can say that the little seed has produced that mighty tree. So with success. It is a little seed-thought and you have to develop it. It won't grow without your help, just as seeds will not grow without your necessary care. All kinds of seeds of power are within you, waiting for you to develop them.

Michelangelo had been working on a statue for many days. He was giving final touches to the statue and was making some minute improvements. A man asked him why he bothered himself with little improvements. **Michelangelo** said – **"Trifles make perfection and perfection is no trifle."**

Warren Mcdonald was a climber and an adventurist. Once when he was climbing a mountain, a huge boulder fell on him. He was seriously injured and both his legs had to be amputated from thigh. After the operation when he opened his eyes, he asked the doctor about the status of his legs. The doctor told him that he won't be able to walk again in his life. Later on this man climbed many high mountains including Mount Kilimanjaro, Africa's tallest peak. In an interview he was asked how he managed in spite of not having his legs. He said that the doctor's words had inspired him. The doctor had said that "I won't be able to walk again, he did not say that I won't be able to climb mountain again". This kind of attitude is needed for doing great things in life.

Harry Lorayne inspires us by saying:

"Make up your mind to win; work toward winning with enthusiasm, and the odds are with you. If you are a person whose goal is merely to avoid failure instead of to attain success, you are looking for the thorns instead of flowers."

Stop worrying, stop moaning, stop groaning, stop complaining – start thinking. Your thought will create your future. Develop courage. Build conviction. Get rid of negative thoughts which generate depression and self-pity. Replace them with positive thoughts. Try to take your mind away from your problems by devoting attention to the needs of others. The golden rule is – "If you want to be happy, make others happy."

When I meet the LL.B first year students for the first time in the class, I tell them that as I look at them I do not see the LL.B first year students but I see in their bright eyes the future Chief Justice of India, the Judges of Supreme Court and High Courts, Law officers, Jurists and Professors of law. I tell them that law students are in no way inferior to the medical or engineering students. They should feel proud of the fact that they are pursuing a course which will lead them to the position of the Chief Justice of India, the judges of Supreme Court and High Courts, eminent lawyers, law officers and jurists. I tell them that if they have any inferiority complex regarding the course it must be thrown in the gutter. I try to make them have faith and confidence in the course they are pursuing and love the course. Gradually they start believing themselves and it is no wonder that many students from our department have become judges, and are serving the nation with pride.

It is the attitude towards works that counts. Those of us who work only for wages will never experience the real joy of working. But when you work with love and consider your work an offering to the Lord, you will find in it a joy forever!

You may be a professor teaching students in a college or a university; you may be a doctor treating patients in a clinic or a hospital; you may be a cook preparing food for five or ten or a hundred people; you may be serving food, sweeping, cleaning or washing dishes; you may be an office assistant or labourer; whatever you do, give it your best; do it in the best way possible, for that is your offering to the Lord. Therefore, work not for wages; work for the love of God! Work for the love of suffering humanity.

There are a hundred ways of doing the same thing – even a simple thing like laying a table, driving a car or peeling vegetables! There are many ways of doing these things, but there is only one way which is the best. We have to do it in the very best way possible, because it is our offering at the lotus-feet of the Lord – nothing less will do for Him.

A shoe company wanted to expand its business to a country in Africa. In order to assess the level of demand for their shoes in that country, the director of the company deputed two separate teams there.

After a study of two months, one team sent a report that there was no market for shoes in that country as no one wore shoes.

The other team concluded that the place had great market potential because no one wore shoes. Once we taught them the habit of wearing shoes and people got accustomed to the habit, then there would be huge demand for shoes in the country.

Once a sad person went to Aristotle and said, "I want to die. I am disappointed with my life." He started crying. Aristotle said, "You should die because it's better to die than live in disappointment." Well, the point which Aristotle wanted to make is that only an optimist can be happy and successful in life. If a person cannot be hopeful, then his life is a waste. If you cannot believe in yourself and be hopeful and face the problems like a man, it is better to die than to put a blot on the human race.

Some people get up in the morning with the hope that things will happen in just the right way so that they will have a good day. They hope the sun will be shining, people will be nice to them, and the lady luck will be on their side. In the process, they surrender control of their well-being to forces over which they have no influence. And this is how they live each day of their life.

Successful people decide what kind of day they are going to have when they get up in the morning. They make a choice; in fact, they make a decision that they are going to have a meaningful and productive day, no matter what. It doesn't matter what the weather is like, whether people are nice to them or how lady luck plays her cards. They know what kind of day they want and they simply go about getting it. They live with the belief that they are in control of their life.

I believe that every competitor is a winner. Nobody who competes can ever be a total loser, because total loser is the person who doesn't dare to try. Every competitor is a winner because he has courage. Just because you have lost the battle doesn't mean you will lose the war.

Things don't change. You change your way of looking. That's all. The meaning of things lies not in the things but in your attitude towards them. We don't see things as they are; we see things as we are. Attitude more than aptitude, will determine our altitude. You have either got a good attitude or a bad one. The choice is up to you.

Thought works! It is a marvellous force. Believe in the power of thought, which comes from God, and use all the strength of your heart, your will to try to materialise that thought. If your will is strong whatever you imagine will be created for you. It is a fact.

Never waste time because it will never come back. If God someday turns away from you, you can call God back by praying to him but you can never call 'time' back. Don't become stagnant in life. Read the self-improvement books or the personality improvement books in your leisure time but do not take the personal-development books as gospel. Read them and take whatever useful ideas you need. Some people feel that they must do everything suggested and take the techniques to extremes. Every book has at least one tool or strategy of benefit. Take what you need and what works for you and discard what doesn't suit you.

Get into the excellent habit of reading something positive and inspirational before you go to bed and as soon as you are awake in the morning. You will soon note the benefits as these thoughts will be supporting you throughout the day.

Carani N Rao says

"The richest place in the world is the graveyard because in it lie all the people who had great ideas which would have made them wealthy and successful but they listened to some pessimistic person who dissuaded them with the word, 'can't' which they believed. Then they took their great ideas along with the belief, 'can't' to their graves."

When you go looking for gold, you move tons of dirt to get an ounce of gold. But you don't look for the dirt; you look only for the gold. We need to focus only on the positive in life instead of looking for what is wrong. Most people find what they look for. If they look for happiness, they get it. If they look for what is wrong with others and situations, they forget to see what is right. When a ship sails the high seas, water that can sink the ship is all around it. But, only that water which gets into the ship can sink a ship. Do not allow yourself to be influenced by the negative forces around you, lest it may sink you.

Let us just concentrate on the words of **Ralph Waldo Emerson**—

"The ancestor of every action is a thought. All thoughts tend to convert themselves into action. A man is so, what he thinks all day long."

All inventors, players, athletes, artists, achievers, those who have succeeded believe in the power of imagination. They first see the positive outcome in their mind and then perform the best. Positive thought, positive visualisation and positive imagination can make good things happen for you. A positive thinker produces positive attitude, positive emotion, positive action, which ultimately leads to get positive result.

How much better it is to use the power of mind than to let it ossify and become like a fossil. So don't be a mental fossil. Be a living tree, constantly spreading out new growth. If you have not achieved anything in life, you may as well consider yourself dead, because like a zombie you are moving toward the valley of death. Everything you do is recorded within yourself. The effect of each positive action is locked up in your brain, and the mental tabloid tendency becomes a powerful potential to bring about any achievement you are seeking.

Harry E. Fosdick said:

"Great things start with a picture held in some person's imagination of what he would like some day to be. Florence Nightingale dreamed of being a nurse. Edison pictured himself as an inventor. Hold the picture of yourself long and steadily in your mind's eye, and you will be drawn toward it."

When your thought is filled with fear, doubt and hate – disbelief in your ability, you suggest your mind, which ultimately takes the spirit to produce the fact, accordingly. You don't act or even if you do act, you do not do it wholeheartedly, confidently, with belief. When your thought is filled with faith, hope and love – belief in your ability, you suggest your mind, which helps to act wholeheartedly, confidently to produce the fact.

According to **James Allen**,

"All that a man achieves is the direct result of his own thoughts. A man can rise, conquer and achieve by lifting up his thoughts. He can only remain weak and abject and miserable by refusing to lift up his thoughts."

Make positive imagination your companion. Most of the people fail even after working hard, because they think and they imagine failure. They fail to teach their subconscious mind for success and listen to their subconscious for failure. To change the fact we need to change the thought. To get success we need to think about success. By approaching problems with a positive frame of mind you can always derive good from them, no matter how difficult they may be.

We can enter a whole new world of our own making by using our incredible imagination, and persistent and focused effort. It's our thoughts that determine who we are. We all create our tomorrow based on what we are thinking today. So simply by changing our thoughts, we can change who we are, and hence every aspect of our life. We become what we contemplate.

Samuel Smiles said:

"Hope is the companion of power, and the mother of success, for who so hopes strongly has within him the gift of miracles."

All that we are is the result of what we have thought. When we think, feel and accept failure we fail, as our actions are regulated to make us fail. When we think, feel and accept success we succeed. Our miserable thoughts make us miserable. Our fearful thoughts make us fearful. Our sickly thoughts make us sick. Whenever a negative thought concerning your ability comes to your mind, deliberately voice a positive thought to cancel it out.

Successful people think about opportunities, affluence, challenge and change. They think about success. Unsuccessful people think about problems, poverty, set-backs, lack and limitation. They think about failure.

Once upon a time there lived three frogs, named 'Neg', 'Neu', and 'Pos'. One day they accidently fell into a pail of milk.

Neg, who was a pessimist cursed life and his bad breaks. He complained, focused his energies on the problem and soon gave up and died.

The second frog Neu, a brilliant mathematician, figured that it could leap to safety if he properly calculated the distance. He computed the algebraic factors of the trajectory, worked out the parabolic and dynamics and then readied himself for the grand leap. He made a valiant attempt to leap out of the milk but he did not get the required thrust. Consequently he fell in the milk once again. He got depressed and died due to frustration.

The third frog, Pos had a positive attitude, a strong will to survive and love for hard work. He directed his energies to the solution rather to the problem. He kept on hopping and kicking. He did not give up. He kept on kicking until he churned the milk into cream, and then into butter. As it became solid he eventually leaped out to safety.

You are living in a world of competition. Competition doesn't throttle you if you have determination. It makes you stronger. You have to do your best every day under all circumstances, and then you can achieve success. But most people don't apply themselves. If you think, "I am done for", you are finished right then; you have already given yourself the decree that you have failed. But if you remain positive and think, "All right, I will succeed", and go on trying you will surely succeed.

It has been rightly said—

If you plant honesty, you will reap trust.
If you plant goodness, you will reap friends.
If you plant humility, you will reap greatness.
If you plant perseverance, you will reap victory.
If you plant consideration, you will reap harmony.
If you plant forgiveness, you will reap reconciliation.
If you plant openness, you will reap intimacy.
If you plant patience, you will reap improvements.
If you plant faith, you will reap miracles.

According to **William James,**

"Faith is the one of the forces by which men live, and the total absence of it means collapse."

Thinking on positive terms helps to get positive results. Our thought process can be detected, controlled, and guarded if it is negative, and can be replaced, erased and substituted by a strong positive thought. Believe that you possess significant reserves of health, energy and endurance and your belief will help create the fact.

Charles Sawyer said:

"Of all the forces that make for a better world, hope is so much indispensable. None is so much powerful as hope — without hope men are only half-alive, with hope they dream, think and work."

It is an established rule that the harder you work, the luckier you get. Wishes are like dreams for they don't come true unless you do something about it. Enthusiasm is the lubricant that oils the machinery of action. It is the passion or enthusiasm that drives us towards our goals, but it is the hard work that yields success. The man, who gets ahead, is the one who does more than necessary and keeps on doing it.

An optimist converts a dream into a reality, but a pessimist converts a reality into a dream. Pessimists believe that neither can good things happen nor can things ever be good. They remain hopeless and faithless. An optimist sees an opportunity in every difficulty, but a pessimist sees a difficulty in every opportunity. An optimist says that rose plant has flowers, but a pessimist says rose flower has thorns. Never think yourself as failing. Never doubt the reality of the mental image.

There was a man who was hungry, and in order that he might appease his hunger, he sat down at a certain place, closed his eyes and began to eat imaginary curry. After a while he was seen with his mouth open, endeavouring to cool his burnt tongue. Somebody asked him what the matter was. He said that in his food there was a very hot chilli. Thereupon a bystander remarked —"Oh, poor fellow, if you had to live on imaginary food, then why not select something far sweeter than hot chilli pepper. As it was your own creation your own doing, your own imagination, why did you not make a better choice.

Barendra Kumar says:

"Positive people think, hope and believe and focus on the best. When they see the cow dung, they think up planting; when they see darkness, they think of stars to look at; when they see the rain, they think up a rainbow. They are not irritated. They understand that with every burden there is blessing and with every blessing there is burden."

Our life has been controlled by our thoughts based on what we listen, what we see, what we accept and what we speak to ourselves. Formulate and stamp indelibly on your mind a mental picture of yourself as succeeding. Hold this picture tenaciously. Never permit it to fade. Your mind will seek to develop this picture as fact. Thoughts have tremendous power. We are the result of our thoughts. We hope, anticipate and expect in our thinking. We imagine, visualise, depict favourable or unfavourable outcome in our thinking. Our desire, in form of thought, later creates the fact.

Fr James Keller says:

"It is better to light a candle, then to curse the darkness."

There are terrible problems the world is confronting today – starvation, poverty, war, violence, religious fanaticism, environmental degradation and more. It is enough to depress the most optimistic among us. And so, even good people exclaim in despair –

"What can I do? How much can we do? Whatever we do, it's not going to be enough!"

True, it may not be enough. But that should be no reason for us to desist from all action. Rather we must do what we can, in the firm faith and belief that, "I can make a difference. I will make a difference". If all of us work in this spirit, the world will surely be a better place.

Each of us has, in his unconscious mind, power and strength and courage past all imaging. Sometimes we fail to use this strength because we do not know it is there. Sometimes we delude ourselves into thinking we do not need it. Sometimes we block it with fear or guilt or tension. An important secret of success is to get firmly based in spiritual understanding, in faith and positive thinking. Then nothing, no matter what, can defeat you. You will have attained immortality and indomitability.

According to **Arnold Fox**,

"If you can't believe wholeheartedly in yourself all at once, that's all right. Don't get down on yourself. Step by step, build your self-love. Remember that belief is the eye of your spirit. What you see is what you get. See yourself as a winner. With your mind's eye see yourself believing enthusiastically in yourself. See yourself saying that you deserve the best life has to offer. Now see yourself seeing it with two eyes in front of your head. Stand in front of a mirror, point your finger at yourself and say, "I believe in You!" Say it with enthusiasm. Look yourself in the eye as you say that over and over, and as you recite your affirmation for belief. Repeat your affirmation for belief at least 20 times a day, all day along. Let your faith in yourself transform you into an iron pillar of belief."

Carani N Rao gives us a formula for happiness in the following words:

Work while you work, and play while you play,
That is the way, to be happy and gay,
Whatever you do, do with your might,
Things done by halves are never done right.
One thing at a time and that done well,
Is the best of all rules, as many can tell.
So work while you work and play while you play,
That is the way, to be happy and gay.

An inspiring story told by **Dr. Harikrishna Devsare** goes like this—

An officer used to defeat his enemies with a meagre number of soldiers and weapons. His name was Nobunaga. Once, he found that his army was lacking the enthusiasm to fight; and another battle was round the corner. He took all soldiers to a temple. He said to them, "I will toss a coin thrice. If the majority of all the tosses are head, we will win, else we will face defeat." He tossed the coin thrice and found head at all times. The soldiers fought bravely and conquered their enemies.

In the grand assembly after the victory, Nobunaga said, "The victory is the result of the coin which had showed head thrice upon tossing. However, the truth is that coin had no 'tail' side. It means that the 'head' increased our confidence and belief in ourselves to such a level that we attained victory."

Optimism is a philosophy based on the belief that basically life is good, that, in the long run, the good in the life overbalances the evil. Also that, in every difficulty, in every pain, there is some good hidden which ultimately makes us more matured and knowledgeable.

Hellen Keller said:

"Keep your face to the sunshine and you can't see the shadow."

Remember the beautiful lines of **Dixie Wilson**—

"Count your garden by the flowers
Never by the leaves that fall.
Count your days by golden hours,
Don't remember clouds at all.
Your night by stars not shadows,
Count your life by smiles, not tears . . .
And, with this on your birthday,
Count your age by friends, not years."

F. Longbridge makes a great point by saying:

"Two men looked through prison bars,
One saw mud; and the other stars."

Once upon a time, there was an eagle's nest that sat on top of the highest mountain peak. A strong wind came and blew an egg out of the eagle's nest and it rolled down the mountain into a valley and ended up in a chicken farm. The mother hen hatched it along with its own eggs.

The eagle chick which was raised along with the chicken by the hen, thought it was a chicken. It walked like a chicken, talked like a chicken, thought like a chicken and dreamed like a chicken. It had no inkling that it was an eagle, a majestic bird, made by God to soar high in the sky. One day it saw its image in a pond and realised that it was an eagle. At that very moment it discarded its chicken identity and soared high into the sky. Similarly, we sometimes consider ourselves as chickens even though we are all eagles, born to fly high in our lives.

According to **Woodrow Wilson,**

"Some of us let great dreams die, but others nourish and protect them, nurse them through bad days till they bring them to the sunshine and light which comes always to those who sincerely hope that their dreams will come true."

The faith healers of India instruct their patients to repeat with full conviction the words, "There is no illness at all". The patients repeat them and this mental suggestion helps to drive off the disease. So if you think yourself to be morally weak, you will actually become so in a short time. Know and believe that you have immense power and then power will come to you.

I am always inspired by the following words of **Norman Vincent Peale—**

"Even as the atmosphere of a room can be changed by air conditioning, so the climate of the mind can be changed by 'thought conditioning'. And a thought can make an enormous difference in how one feels mentally, emotionally, and physically. Certainly to have a great day every day it helps to think great thought and to concentrate on at least one great thought every day."

**

6

Don't Get Discouraged by Criticism

A cow is never criticised by anyone but it remains a cow all its life. If you have never been criticised in your life it means you have never done anything worthwhile and great. A wall is never criticised but it remains a wall all its life. So the only way to avoid criticism is to become a dead wall or a cow.

Criticism is a conclusive evidence that people are noticing you and giving importance to you and to your work. It is a proof that you are being seriously monitored by people and people are not finding it to be wastage of time to think about you and your activities. So instead of getting discouraged by criticism we must get encouraged by criticism. The world is so busy that no one has the time to think about somebody else. You must thank the critics that at least they do not mind spending their precious time in thinking about you and commenting on your work.

The critics' intolerance and jealousy are at the back of most criticism and they derive a kind of perverted or sadistic joy by finding fault with others. The only way to avoid criticism is to do nothing. It is thousand times easier to criticise than to create. That is why critics are never problem solvers. If you are truly disturbed by their criticism it seems you are lacking in self-confidence. If you are conscious of your duty and if you are self-confident, the unjust criticism of others will not affect you at all.

You can follow the advice of **Edward Gibbon.** He said:

"I never make the mistake of arguing with people for whose opinions I have no respect."

However, well you may have accomplished the task, you are likely to invite criticism of some kind or other. Criticism is only a warning bell calling you to be alert. To be absolutely free from criticism, one should never say anything, never do anything, and never become anything.

Always remember that a successful man is he, who can lay firm foundation with the bricks that others throw at him.

Once a visitor said to **Swami Ramatirtha**, "People do not like you."

Swami Ramatirtha replied, **"When they like an apple they swallow it. When they like a plum they also do the same. If they like meat they swallow it too. Good that they don't like me. If they had liked me, they would have also swallowed me!"**

One of my students in the LL.B class was often criticised by his friends for participating in various competitions such as moot-court, debates, extempore, etc., even though he did not have good communication skills. People used to laugh at him whenever he made pronunciation mistakes and other grammatical mistakes in his communication. One day he came to me and narrated to me his problem. I said, "Do not pay heed to those criticisms and comments. You are far better than those students who out of fear of criticism do not participate and thus remain stagnant in their lives. With every competition you are progressing and developing yourself and a day will come when you will become excellent in your communication. Remember that in the long run you will be the gainer and your critics the losers."

My prediction came true and that student is now a teacher of law teaching in a law college. He is a very popular teacher and appreciated for his oratory skills.

Jean Sibelius said:

"Pay no attention to what the critics say. A statue has never been erected in honour of a critic."

Indian saint **Ramanujcharya's** words are full of wisdom. He says:

"Purity of though leads to purity of action. Do not find fault in others. No one is perfect and none is competent to talk

about the weakness of another. Goodness consists in service to others and this means active help."

Once I was travelling by train to my university. In my compartment were some young boys who were making derogatory comments about Gandhiji. They were taking pride in their criticism against Gandhiji and seemed to be showing off their deep knowledge about the father of our nation. At last it was beyond my toleration limit and I protested. I said, "Are you qualified enough to pass comment on this great man? What is your qualification? Have you done a research on Gandhiji? From where have you got these derogatory facts about Gandhiji? What is the source of your information? What is the evidence that the source of your information is true and authentic? Are you a contemporary of Gandhiji? Was he your friend, that you know these things about him? My dear friend, you are a worm crawling in the dust and you are passing comment on the Mount Everest. First reach that height which these great men have scaled and then think of criticising these great men."

My sudden outburst stumped them and they realised their mistakes. One of them said, "Sir, today you have opened my eyes. Our criticism against Gandhiji was like a 'sieve' telling to the needle that you have a hole in you. I will try to implement the lesson I have learnt today from you throughout my life."

John Mason said:

"Nobody can make you feel average without your permission. Ingratitude and criticism are going to come. They are part of the price you pay for leaping past mediocrity."

When I had joined the law course as a student, I had to face a lot of criticism. People said that I had joined law as there was nothing else to do in life. Some said that I was not getting job anywhere and that was the reason for my joining law. They were not aware of the fact that it was the divine will which made me join the law course. Therefore, I did not pay much heed to the criticisms and humiliations targeted at me. I knew what my mission was and the task which I had to accomplish. I knew there was no shortcut to reach my goal. From the very first day of my joining law I made up my mind to study minimum 8 hours everyday so that I could gain complete mastery over the subjects. I knew that at the top of the mountain there is place for only one person and I wanted to be that person. After five years I was there, receiving the gold medal from the Governor of West Bengal for securing first class first rank in the university with record marks. My labour and hard work for the last five years had borne fruit and I was happy and satisfied in reaching the first step of my mission.

Oscar wilde's suggestion is worth noting—

"Don't waste time responding to your critics, because you owe nothing to them."

There was a person who bought an amazing parrot. It could sing all the songs sung by Lata Mangeskar, the famous singer of India. He invited his friends to listen to the songs sung by this amazing parrot. After the parrot sang some songs, the crowd applauded except one person. The owner of the parrot went to that man and said "You did not applaud. Didn't you find anything amazing about this parrot? The man said, "Yes I found one thing amazing. Your parrot cannot sing the songs of Asha Bhonsle."

Critics may say anything. But if you are convinced that their words are baseless, you may ignore them. You may pray to God, "O Lord, make me deaf to their harsh criticism."

No one has totally escaped criticism. When Einstein's Theory of Relativity was published scientists ridiculed it as a foolish theory. Some people, regarded as wise and intelligent by others, entertain the feeling that to acknowledge the qualities of others is to admit their own inadequacy and they refrain from any kind of appreciation of others, though they will not hesitate to direct any criticism, well-founded or ill-founded.

Once during my interview for the post of lecturer, when I placed my publications before the expert committee, one of the experts just scanned my article published in one of the prestigious journals for a few seconds and then threw the journal away, saying what a disgusting and low standard article I had written. He further said that such article should have never been published and should be thrown in the gutter. It was a great humiliation for me. But I kept my calm and cool because I had confidence in the quality of my article and I was sure that the expert had some ulterior motive. I just said that my article was selected by the editorial board of the journal and the editorial board comprised retired judges and prominent High Court lawyers. So if the article was that bad it would not have been selected for publication by these experts of the editorial board. Well my answer failed to convince the expert and I was not selected in that interview.

Just a few days after this interview, I got an offer from one of the leading publishing houses for writing a book for them. They said that they were so impressed by a particular article of mine in a journal that they considered me the fittest person to write a book for them. The article which impressed the publishing house was the same article which the 'expert' had labelled 'low standard' in the interview. I was happy because I had got my reward.

So, the point is the critics will go on criticising and we shall have to move on with our work in spite of criticism. If you have faith in your ability and your work you will certainly get your reward, maybe not in the short run but surely in the long run.

Some people have made a career out of criticising. They will find fault with every person and every situation. We should learn to expect ingratitude. Jesus himself was thanked by only one out of ten lepers he had healed.

There is one guaranteed formula for failure, and that is to try to please everyone. We should never throw mud because if you do, you may hit your mark but you will have dirty hands. Give so much time to the improvement of yourself that you have no time to criticise others.

I had given eight volumes of 'The Complete Works of Swami Vivekananda' to a student to read. After about a month when he returned the books to me, I asked him what he learnt from the books. He said that he came to know from the book that Swami Vivekananda was a smoker. I asked him what about Swamiji's speech in the Parliament of Religions in Chicago? What about his works in America? What about his works on Karma Yoga, Raj Yoga, and Bhakti Yoga? What about his intense patriotism? I said, "My dear, from a mine full of diamonds you have picked up some very cheap pebbles."

It has been rightly said by **Tynan**: **"A critic is a man who knows the way but can't drive a car."** The nature of critics is beautifully illustrated by the following story which I read in **Shiv Khera's** book 'You can Win'.

Robert Fulton invented the steamboat. He displayed his new invention on the banks of Hudson River. Among the crowd who had gather around to observe the steamboat were some critics. They commented that it would never start. But suddenly the steamboat started and zoomed off. As it made its way down the river the people asked the critics, "You said it will never start but it going with such great speed." The critics remarked, "Well it may have started but now it is not going to stop."

There was a great leader who was addressing a huge public rally favouring his presidential election campaign, when a heckler arose from the crowd and shouted at him, "Today you want to be the president of this country. But own up to the truth about your past to this crowd. Is it not true that a few years ago, you were just a cobbler?"

The great leader was unmoved by this outburst. He smiled and said, "It is true I was just a cobbler; but I am proud to say I cobbled well!"

The crowd heard his answer and broke into thunderous applause. They saw a man before them who embodied the true sense of duty – whatever he did, he did well. Whatever he will be given to do, he will do well.

**

7

Honesty is Still the Best Policy

Some years back I was returning from Howrah by local train. I was reading a book and was lost in my own world. Suddenly I found out that there was some commotion in the compartment. I saw that some ticket checkers had entrained and they were checking the tickets of the passengers. One old poor lady was detained by them for not having ticket in her possession and they were demanding fine from her. After some arguments she paid Rs. 50 to the ticket checkers. At last they came to me and asked for my ticket. As I put my hand in my pocket to search for the ticket I realised that I had accidently dropped the ticket somewhere. Not only that to add to my misfortune I had no money to pay the fine. I told them the truth and said that I have the ATM card with me and after getting down at Chinsurah I will draw the money from the ATM booth and pay the requisite fine. The ticket checkers said that they would get down at the next station and also said that I need not to pay any fine as they believed me and asked me to be a little more careful.

They got down at the next station but my conscience continued to prick me. I felt that there was no difference between me and that old poor lady who had to pay a fine for not possessing the ticket. I was also an offender because I didn't possess the ticket. It did not matter whether I did not buy any ticket or I had lost the ticket. Instead of going to Chinsurah I went back to the station where the checkers had got down. I went to the nearby ATM booth and drew the fine amount and went to the chamber of ticket checkers at the station. Luckily I found the same ticket checkers sitting there. They were surprised to see me and asked me the reason for coming. I said that I had come to pay the fine. They felt as if they were struck by lightning. They could not believe their ears. I repeated that I had come to pay the fine.

They offered me a chair to sit down and a little later they brought tea and snacks for me. I was also offered sweets as if I was some special guest They said that they were really pleased with my honesty and called me incarnation of Mahatma Gandhi. In my mind I was thinking that so much respect was being shown to an 'offender' only because of honesty. That day I realised the power and strength of the word 'Honesty'.

Listen to what **John Mason** has to say on this point—

"Lie has no legs. It has to be supported by other lies. There is no substitute for truth. There is no acceptable replacement for honesty. There is no valid excuse for dishonesty, and nothing shows like a white lie. It may seem that a lie has taken care of the present, but it has no future. Hope built on a lie is always the beginning of loss – a shady person never produces a bright life."

Sadhu Navalrai, a pillar of the Sindhi community, rose to become the deputy collector of a district – the highest civil service post to which an Indian could be elevated under the British regime. As a deputy collector, he had magisterial duties too, adjudicating civil cases brought before him. One fine day his own father was brought before him. The old man had transported opium without paying octroi tax. He was confident that he could get away with it as his son was the deputy collector. He secretly smiled to himself as his case was presented before his son, quite sure that he would be let off lightly. But to his surprise he was awarded the maximum punishment. For Sadhu Navalraj, justice and honesty came first and then his father.

To be excellent, be honest. Each time you are honest, you propel yourself toward greater success. Each time you lie, even a little white lie, you push yourself toward failure. There is no degree of honesty. There is no power on earth more overpowering than the truth.

Once I went to a park in Chandannagar with my wife and two sons aged 5 years 3 months and 3 years. The sign at the ticket counter read: "No ticket required for children under the age 5". I bought three tickets, one each for myself, my wife and my elder son aged 5 years 3 months. The person at the ticket counter asked me about the age of my elder son. I said he is 5 years and 3 months old. The person at the ticket counter was amazed and astonished. He said if you had not told me, I would have never known. You could have saved 20 rupees easily if you had passed off your son as under 5. I said, my dear friend, it is true that if I had not told you his age you would never come to know, but the problem is my son would know that his father had lied and passed him off as under 5. I do not want my son to become a liar and dishonest person.

After visiting the park when I was coming out of the park the person at the ticket counter came to me and said, "Sir, today you have taught me a great lesson of honesty."

According to **Pearl Buck**,

"Truth is always exciting. Speak it, then. Life is dull without it."

Once Swami Vivekananda, known as Narendra during his school days, was talking animatedly to his friends during a class recess. Meanwhile, the teacher had entered the classroom and begun to teach his subject. But the students were too absorbed in Narendra's story to pay any attention to the lesson. After some time had passed, the teacher heard the whispering and understood what was going on! Visibly annoyed, he asked each student what he had been lecturing on. None could answer. But Narendra was remarkably talented. His mind could work simultaneously on two planes. While he had engaged one part of his mind in talking he had kept the other half on the lesson, so when the teacher asked him that question, he answered correctly. Quite nonplussed, the teacher inquired who had been talking so long. Everybody pointed at Narendra, but the teacher refused to believe them. He then asked all students except Narendra to stand up on the bench. Narendra also joined his friends and stood up. The teacher asked him to sit down. But Narendra replied, "No sir, I must also stand up because it was I who was talking to them." The teacher was quite impressed by Narendra's honesty and forgave him and his friends.

In his book 'Freedom is not Free' Shiv Khera has written that an honest citizen must be prepared to forfeit one's life. Well, that may be true but I feel it is better to forfeit our lives in pursuit of honesty than to live a life of dishonesty and die thousand times. Life must not be long, it must be worthy. Swami Vivekananda's life was not a long one. He died at the age of 39 but it was such a significant and worthy life. He left this world with dignity after completing his mission of life. So it does not matter if you have to sacrifice your life in upholding honesty. That death will be far-far better and dignified than treading on the path of dishonesty and dying like a worm in the gutter.

There was a competition going on in a club. The prize would go to the person who said the biggest lie. Everybody was trying to outshine others by telling bigger lie. Then a dispute started among the competitors as to whose lie was the biggest one. At that moment a so-called 'godman' came inside the club and asked what the problem was. After listening to them he said that they should not be holding such kind of competition where the requirement for winning prize was based on telling lies. He then said that in his life he had never spoken any lie and expected other people to follow his example. Suddenly, a person from the crowd said – "Well, give the prize to the 'godman'. His lie is unmatchable."

Honesty is a great force. Honesty means integration of the three aspects of personality – thought, speech and deed. For instance, when you give a promise to anyone, honesty demands that you act accordingly or at least make a sincere attempt to act according to the promise. Otherwise, it is dishonesty or deceit.

Dishonesty is a great enemy within us which destroys us in the long run. A jellyfish sometimes swallows a snail and since the snail is protected in the shell, it remains alive. But for its survival, it needs food. So it starts eating the jellyfish from inside and keeps growing till it consumes the entire jellyfish. Dishonesty is similar to the snail inside the jellyfish. It eats you from inside and one day you are finished.

Einstein's dedication to truthfulness was similar to Mahatma Gandhi's. The occasional pang of conscience regarding a moral issue remained with him for a long time. Like Gandhiji, Einstein dedicated himself to the work of his chosen path. It is well-known that science was Einstein's refuge in times of difficulty and sorrow and that from youth he was proficient in his study and work habits. In his early days at the Patent Office, he performed his patent investigations so efficiently that he was left with a few hours of free time. Rather than socialise or fritter away these precious hours, he spent them writing down his calculation and research on a piece of paper. He quickly hid this work in a nearby drawer whenever he heard someone approaching. This action bothered his conscience even after he became famous and he continued to feel remorseful about it. ["Albert Einstein, His human side", By Swami Tathagatananda]

There is another beautiful story told by **Carani. N Rao**, which highlights in a very simple way how honesty is ultimately rewarded. The story goes like this—

An emperor in the Far East was growing old and realised it was time to choose his successor. Instead of choosing one of his assistants or his children he decided something different. He called all the young people in the kingdom together, one day. He said, "It is time for me to step down and choose the next emperor. I have decided to choose one of you." The children were shocked. But the emperor continued, "I am going to give each one of you a seed today, one very special seed. I want you to plant the seed, water it and come back here after one year from today with what you have grown from this one seed. I will then judge the plants that you bring and the one I choose will be the next emperor."

One boy named Ling was there that day and he, like the others, received a seed. He went home and excitedly told his mother the story. She helped him get a pot and planting soil and he planted the seed and watered it carefully. Every day, he would water it and watch to see if it had grown.

After about three weeks, some of the other youths began to talk about their seeds and the plants that were beginning to grow. Ling kept checking his seed, but nothing ever grew. Three weeks, four weeks, five weeks went by. Still nothing had happened. By now, others were talking about their plants, but Ling did not have plant, and he felt like a failure. Six months went by, still nothing in Ling's pot. Everyone else had trees and tall plants, but he had nothing. However, Ling did not say anything to his friends. He just kept waiting for his seed to grow.

A year finally went by and all the youths of the kingdom brought their plants to the emperor for inspection. Ling reluctantly took his empty pot to the palace. When Ling arrived, he was amazed at the variety of plants grown by the other youths. They were beautiful, in all shapes and sizes. Ling put his empty pot on the floor and many of the other youths laughed at him. A few felt sorry for him and just said, "Hey, nice try."

When the emperor arrived, he surveyed the room and greeted the young people.

Ling just tried to hide in the back. "My God, what great plants, trees and flowers you have grown," said the emperor. "Today one of you will be appointed the next emperor!" All of a sudden the emperor spotted Ling at the back of the room with his empty pot. He ordered his guards to bring him to the front. Ling was terrified and thought, "The emperor knows I am a failure! Maybe he will have killed me!" When Ling got to the front, the emperor asked his name. "My name is Ling," he replied. All the other young boys were laughing and making fun of him.

The emperor asked everyone to keep quit. He looked at Ling and then announced to the crowd, "Behold your new emperor! His name is Ling!" Ling couldn't believe it.

Ling couldn't even grow his seed. How could he be the new emperor? Asked the gathered youths. The emperor said, "One year ago today, I gave everyone here a seed. I told you to take the seed, plant it, water it and bring it back to me today. But I gave you all ***boiled seeds which would not grow****. All of you, except Ling, have brought me trees and plants and flowers.* ***When you found that the seed would not grow, you substituted another seed for the one I gave you.*** *Ling was the only one with* ***the courage and honesty*** *to bring me a pot with my seed in it. Therefore, he is the one who will be the new emperor."*

Norman Vincent Peale says:

"Make no mistake about it; any kind of dishonesty cripples, and the first thing you lose is freedom. One has to lie to cover up and soon becomes entangled in lies. An entangled person cannot be free. The honest person is the free person."

There was a judge whose son was brought to his court on murder charges. All the evidences were against the young man and it became clear at the end of the trial that the young man had indeed committed the crime. The learned justice was also convinced that his son had indeed committed the murder. With heavy heart the learned justice went home to write the sentence. His wife pleaded with him to spare the life of their only son, but he knew his duty as upholder of the law. On the following day he pronounced the death sentence on his only son; on the same evening, he died of a massive heart attack. It was a great example of being honest and sincere to one's duty.

K. Saranya tells us a thought-provoking story which in a very special way highlights the importance of honesty in our lives. The story goes like this—

Prabakar, at a very early age, lost his parents during an epidemic. None of his relatives helped him during the most difficult times. He worked hard as a petty clerk and earned small salary. After long years of sincere work, he built up his own business and became rich. Thus he learnt the value of money.

Prabakar had a son, Shankar. He was loved by Prabakar and his wife Rathi very much. Prabakar wanted Shankar to realise the value of money. He was put in a school but he did not progress much since he was not serious about education. Before Shankar was taken into his own business, Prabakar wanted him to work somewhere and earn money out of his own toil.

One day Prabakar called Shankar and advised him to try for a job or work somewhere and earn money. It was the responsibility of Shankar to visit various offices and business centres seeking a job. Unfortunately, he was unable to get a job in spite of his best efforts. It was a discouragement to Shankar. He felt ashamed to see his father who often enquired about his getting a job or work to earn money.

Rathi was sad to see the plight of Shankar. Without Prabakar's knowledge, Rathi called Shankar, spoke to him lovingly and told him, "My dear son, don't worry. Take this fifty rupees and tell your father that you have earned this money by doing some work in the market. Once your father is convinced that you have earned the money he would not bother you later."

Shankar thought it was a good idea. He took the money with great relief and approached his father. Stretching the currency note to his father he said, "Father, I have done some work in the market place today and earned this fifty rupees."

Shankar felt that his father Prabakar would be happy. Contrary to his expectation Prabakar threw the currency note into fire. Though the fifty rupees was lost in a moment, Shankar was not upset, and Prabakar could understand what was in the mind of Shankar.

Unable to study the mind of his father, Shankar approached his mother. To see that Shankar was not disappointed, Rathi gave him another fifty rupee note and advised him to approach his father once again. Shankar approached his father for the second time and said, "Father, I have earned another fifty rupees by doing a part time job." Prabakar looked into his eyes and once again threw the currency note into the fire. Shankar was puzzled. He began thinking about the attitude of his father.

Now Shankar did not want to approach his mother once again. He decided to honestly do some work and earn money. He went and tried seriously and at last he was lucky enough to get a part time work in a small shop. For his work from morning to evening he was paid Rs. 50. Now Shankar was very happy that out of his own toil he could earn some money. With satisfaction, he approached his father and showed him the Fifty Rupee note which he earned out of hard work. As usual Prabakar threw the currency note into the fire for the third time. Now Shankar was totally upset and could not tolerate his hard earned money being burnt away in the fire. In great anger he cried out, "Father, how cruel are you? For ten hours I worked hard and earned this money. Without any thought, you have thrown it into the fire. I cannot tolerate this." Tears rolled down the cheeks of Shankar and he simply cried without relief.

Prabakar smiled, embraced Shankar and told him lovingly, "My dear son, I knew what all happened. Earlier your mother gave you money and you were not upset when it was thrown into fire. But today you are in tears because it is your hard earned money. My son, this is the difference between the money got easily and money earned out of hard work. Since you have understood the value of money, I will take you into my business right from tomorrow." Thus saying Prabakar wiped away the tears of Shankar and patted him on his back. [Wisdom, 2009, January issue]

The moral of the story is that you realise the value of money only when it is earned honestly out of hard work.

HEIGHT OF DISHONESTY: Some years back one of my father's colleagues was transferred from All India Radio, Itanagar, in Arunachal Pradesh to All India Radio, Chinsurah in West Bengal. Due to some reasons he was not paid the travelling allowance. He was released from the Itanagar office for joining the Chinsurah office. He came to Chinsurah but did not join the Chinsurah office for six months. Instead he joined some private company and made lot of money and enjoyed himself. After 6 months he came to join the All India Radio, Chinsurah office and resume his duties.

The authorities at Chinsurah office said, "You were released from the Itanagar office six months back and since you were on unauthorised leave, your service has been discontinued and you will not get the salary for the last six months."

The person said, "This is not fair. I was not on unauthorised leave. Actually I am a very poor person and I did not have the money to travel by air, or train or bus from Arunachal Pradesh.

So six months back I had started my journey on foot. I used to walk ten kilometres everyday and after six months I was able to cover the entire distance from Itanagar to Chinsurah. This morning itself I reached Chinsurah and without wasting any time I came here to join and resume my duties."

The authorities were stunned by his reply and were rendered speechless.

**

8

Live for Others

It is said that the happiness and pleasure you get by doing some services to others is the best kind of bliss. Generally people are careless and very rarely someone comes ahead from amongst the crowd to rush the injured to the hospital or come to the rescue of a dying person. There is no such ingredient in wealth that can give you bliss or happiness. But if you are prepared to spend your wealth in helping the needy and the poor, certainly the bliss and happiness will be yours unasked.

Only those people are really happy who have risen above their selfishness and devote themselves for helping others. This certainly gives inner happiness besides name and fame.

I like the beautiful words of **William Arthur Dunkerley**:

"Art thou lonely, O my brother?
Share thy little with another!
Stretch a hand to one unfriended,
And the loneliness is ended . ."

Do good deed every day or at least think of good deeds every day. You should try this mantra in your life and see its magnetic influence. Some people may think that it is beyond their means. But no, that is certainly not; you need not bestow wealth, money or riches to spread happiness. It is through your sweet words coming straight from the heart that you may be able to distribute happiness to those who may come in your contact. Besides, you may also be able to do some service physically to the injured and sick. That is why Gandhiji once wrote in the autograph copy of a

British soldier: "It does not cost to be kind". Your motto should be, "Get happiness by spreading happiness amongst others".

I have a friend who is well known for his magnanimity and kindness of heart. Whatever money he gets from his meagre salary he spends most of it in helping poor students and he himself lives from hand to mouth. It happened many times in his life that as he passed through some street and saw some poor beggars lying half-asleep, with his knees bent upwards in his stomach because of cold, my friend could not help himself but took off his blanket and covered the poor beggar with the same and went away shivering himself.

Remember to give or donate while you are living in this world. You will be appreciated and remembered for your charity only when you donate while living, otherwise your position will be like the position of the pig in the following story as told by **A.P. Periera**—

Once upon a time there lived a pig. He always lamented his lack of popularity. He complained that people were always speaking well of the cow, but no one ever had a good word for him. True the cow gave milk and cream, but he maintained, pigs gave more: they provided man with bacon and ham, and bristles for brushes. He demanded the reason for such lack of appreciation. The cow thought for a while, then remarked, "It may be that people like me because I give milk while I am living while you give everything only after you are dead."

To give happiness to others with your loving words is like lighting a candle with another candle. As the light of candle does not become less by lighting another candle, similarly by touching the heart of another individual with your pleasant words you do not lose anything. Rather you also get happiness in return. Do not seek to serve others to prove your superiority. This brings disgrace to you, and it degrades those whom you serve in this spirit. It destroys the very spirit and concept of service.

The only way to be happy is to make others happy. You will never be so close to anyone as when you are doing something for them with no other motive than their happiness or welfare. To talk of renunciation and worship of God while ignoring human suffering is futile for God loves those who love the poor and the helpless ones.

Swami Vivekananda points out to us in his roaring voice:

"This life is short, the vanities of the world are transient, but they alone live who live for others, the rest are more dead than alive."

Service makes us evolve spiritually, and helps us realise in deeds of daily life, the great truth of the brotherhood of all creation. Such service helps us on the path of spiritual advancement. It leads us towards God-realisation. It awakens the divine within us. Do not speak harsh words to the people you serve. A sense of identification is very essential to the spirit of true service. Do not criticise or condemn others. Service is meant to purify the mind, the heart and the intellect, and to move us on the path of God-realisation.

Once when plague broke out, Swami Vivekananda started helping and tending to the sick in hospital. Someone asked him, "Swamiji, you are not a doctor. You cannot do a whole lot for the sick. You should really be out there praying for these people." Swamiji replied, "What I am doing is my prayer. What you do in temples are only rituals."

John Wesley gives us a wonderful philosophy to be happy. He says:

"Do all the good you can
By all the means you can
In all the ways you can
At all times you can
To all the people you can
As long as ever you can."

Love is a divine quality. It can enable us to create a halo of peace, amity and cheer all around us. Unfortunately, we are not able to curb our selfish tendencies. We forget that the edifice of peace and happiness is raised on the foundation of love, which call for a great deal of self-sacrifice.

Swami Sivananda says:

"Even if one has no money to help others, he can help them amply with good thoughts. Kind, encouraging words infuse new strength and vitality in the distressed people. One can conquer the whole world through love, humility and service."

Let me tell you here a beautiful story as told by **Mahatma Devesh Bhikshu**. The story goes like this—

Once upon a time a king was ruling in a country. He had a son of tender age. The king loved his son very much and did all what he could to keep his son happy with all the comforts of life. The child had all what he wanted, as in the beautiful rooms of the palace, all kinds of comforts and luxuries were provided. There was abundance of everything – books, artistic paintings, entertainment books, pictorial as well as novels, stories, etc., besides the many kinds of mechanical toys in large numbers. He was also provided with a fine horse for riding. For the son of the king, many learned pundits and educationists were kept. Many colleagues and servants were engaged to keep the prince happy. Yet with all these, the prince remained unhappy, dissatisfied and sad all the while. He was always cross wherever he went and would insist on something or the other.

At last, a learned man came to the court of the king and seeing the unhappy face of the prince, he spoke thus: "Oh king! The shadow of dissatisfaction on the face of the prince can be easily changed into smile. But for doing so, I would want reward I may ask for." The king at once agreed to his condition, saying that he would gladly give him the reward of his liking. But something to be done to make the prince happy. The learned man took the prince to a room all alone. There he wrote something on a piece of paper with some white substance. Then he handed over a candle to the prince and asked him to light it. Having lighted the candle, he told the prince, "Take hold of the paper in one hand and heat it over the lighted candle. Now try to read what is written." So saying, the learned man left. The prince did as he was told. As soon as the heat reached the paper, blue and beautiful words appeared on the paper, on which it was written—"Be kind to someone everyday". The prince acted on these words and thus he became the happiest individual throughout the kingdom.

A **Chinese saying** goes like this—

If you want to be happy for an hour, go and take a nap,
If you want to be happy for a day, go out for a picnic,
If you want to be happy for a month, go and get married,
If you want to be happy for a year, inherit a fortune,
But if you want to be happy all your life, then go and help others."

If our hands become selfish and assert them as different from the other parts of the body and begin to argue this way, "Look here, I am the right hand. I do all sorts of labour, why should the whole body partake of what is earned by sweating drudgery. Should the food earned by my toil be given to the stomach and thence to all other organs? No, no, I will have everything to myself." Then in order to carry into effect this selfish idea, there is no other way for the hand but to take that food and inoculate or inject it into its skin. Will that be beneficial to the hand? Will the hand succeed that way? Never!

According to **Shiv Khera**,

"Hands that serve humanity are a lot better than lips that just talk of divinity."

You should always serve unconditionally and lovingly. Don't serve others with an ulterior motive – to convert them to your ideology; to force them to follow your beliefs; or to support your political party. Be grateful to those who give you the opportunity to serve them. You are not doing favour to them – they are offering you the chance to show your gratitude to the God. Seek no reward for your service nor recognition from the world. Serve silently. Do not serve for show or publicity; let the right hand not know what your left hand gives away. Do not seek to serve or charity for name, fame, popularity, or publicity. Give and serve in the spirit of love and sympathy for all. Serve others in the spirit of serving God. There is no religion higher than the religion of unity and love, of service and sacrifice.

Similarly, remember that all the world is one body. Your body is simply like the hand or the finger. In order that you may succeed, you should not look upon yourself as separate and distinct from the self of the whole world. In order that the hand may prosper, it must realise that its interests are identical with those of the whole world. In other words, the hand must not feel and realise that its self is not confined within the small area beyond the wrist, but must practically feel itself as identical and one with the self of the whole system.

Lord Lawrence, the Governor General of India was boarding a ship bound for India. Also travelling on the ship was a lady with a baby. She neglected her child to such extent that it was practically crying day and night. This became a source of great annoyance to the passengers and some of them even threatened to throw the child overboard. The mother was obviously neglecting her duty. But Lord Lawrence decided to do something which no one thought of doing. He took the baby from the mother and began to laugh and play with it. The happy and contented baby soon stopped crying. The mother was ashamed of herself, for a great man had taught her how to do her duty well!

German doctor Albert Schweitzer was committed to serve and treat people in West Africa. He believed that all life is precious and must be cared for. He served the masses and was awarded Nobel Peace Prize in 1952.

Florence Nightingale was committed to serve the people. She changed the nursing profession to make it meaningful, useful and respectable.

The American President Cleveland was travelling by train once. His biographer, Richard Gilder, also boarded the same train. On being told that the president was travelling in the train, Gilder went in search of him, for he had something important to communicate to the president. But a long and thorough search up and down the train failed to reveal the presence of the president in any one of the crowded coaches. Puzzled Gilder went into the baggage car to question the conductor. There, to his great surprise found the nation's Chief Executive seated on a wooden crate! A woman with a baby had boarded the train, and Cleveland had offered his seat to her.

There should be no room for cruelty in our hearts. Cruelty is an animal trait. It degrades a man to the level of a beast. A person harbouring cruel inclinations in his heart does not deserve to be called a human being. He is a beast masquerading as a human being.

Gandhiji was appalled when he learnt, in Kolkata, of the sacrifice of animals to appease Goddess Kali. He wrote, **"To my mind the life of a lamb is no less precious than that of a human being. I hold that the more helpless a creature, the more entitled it is to protection by man, from the cruelty to man."**

There is a direct link between sacrifice and happiness, because without one, it is just not possible to understand the value of the other. The more you are able to sacrifice your comforts and practice austerity and renunciation of your own free will, the more happiness and joy you are likely to feel in your heart.

You should remember that if you have not fed a poor man today, or offered water to a thirsty one, or offered a piece of cloth to a naked one, or uttered a word of comfort to someone in distress, you have wasted your day. We keep on wasting day after day if we neglect the opportunity to save or serve others, to bring comfort to the depressed, to help the poor and the underprivileged, to bring joy into the lives of joyless ones.

Sadhu Vaswani tells us a beautiful story to highlight the philosophy of living for others. The story goes like this—

A merchant was travelling to a distant town, accompanied by his horse and donkey. He himself rode the horse, while the donkey was laden with all the merchandise. The horse skipped along merrily, feeling very proud. The donkey was suffering from a chill, and could barely move with the heavy burden on his back. It cried out to the horse, "Dear brother, take a little burden off my back, just for today! Give me some relief from the pain I have to endure."

The horse laughed haughtily and said, "You are just a donkey and it is your lot to carry burdens. As for me, I am the chosen beast of my master. How can I carry your burden?"

The donkey was so broken-hearted by this jeer that it fell down and died on the spot. Shocked by this, the merchant jumped off from the horse's back and tried to revive the donkey. When he realised that he could do nothing he sighed sadly and loaded all the merchandise on to the horse's back. And then feeling sorry for the donkey he decided that he would take it with him and give it a decent burial, instead of abandoning it there. So the dead donkey was also loaded on the horse's back, and the merchant walked sadly beside the horse.

The horse was ashamed of itself and bitterly repented. "I wish I had taken a little burden from the donkey when it begged me to help him," the horse thought. "It would have saved the life of the donkey and I would have been spared this burden too."

Whenever a man falls out of harmony with the nature he suffers; the very moment you realise your unity with fellow-beings, all prosperity is yours. **Swami Ram Tirtha** tells us a beautiful story to highlight this point. The story goes as follows:

A king went into a forest on a hunting expedition. In the heat of the chase the king became separated from his companions. Under the scorching rays of the burning sun, he felt very thirsty. He found in the woods a small garden. He went into the garden, but being in his sportsman's dress the gardener could not recognise him, the poor village gardener having not seen the king in person before. The king asked the gardener to bring him something to drink as he was very thirsty. The gardener went straight into the garden, took some pomegranates, squeezed out the juice and brought a big cup full of it to the king. The king gulped it down, but it did not quench his parching thirst entirely. The king asked him to bring another cup of pomegranate juice. The gardener went for it. When the gardener had left the king's presence, the king began to reflect with himself, "This garden seems to be very rich; in half-a-minute the man could bring me a large cup full of the fresh juice; a heavy income-tax ought to be levied on the owner of such a flourishing concern, etc."

On the other hand the gardener delayed and delayed, did not return to the king even in an hour. The king began to wonder, "How is it that when I first asked him to bring me something to drink, he brought that pomegranate juice in less than a minute, and now he has been squeezing out the juice of pomegranates for about an hour and the cup is not full yet. How is that?" After one hour the cup was brought to the king, but not brimful. The king asked the reason why the cup was somewhat empty, whereas he filled the cup so soon at first. The gardener who was a sage replied, "Our king had very good intentions when I went out to bring you the first cup of pomegranate juice, and when I went out to bring you the second cup, our king's kind, benevolent nature must have changed. I can give no other explanation for such a sudden change in the rich nature of my pomegranates." The king reflected within himself, and lo! The statement was perfectly right. When the king had first stepped into the garden, he was very charitably disposed to and full of love for the people there, thinking in his mind that they were very poor and needed help, but when the old man had brought him one cup of pomegranate juice in so short a time, the king's mind had changed and ties altered. The falling out of tune with nature on the king's part affected the pomegranates in the garden. The moment the law of love was violated by the king that very moment the trees held back the juice from him.

The truth is undeniable that so long as you are in perfect harmony with the nature, so long as your mind is in tune with the universe and you are feeling and realising your oneness with each and all, all the circumstances and surroundings, even winds and waves, will be in your favour. The very moment you are at discord with the 'All' that very moment your friends and relatives will turn against you, that very moment you will make the whole world stand up in arms against you. Understand this divine law of love and practice it. Love is a vital principle of success.

Generally, people think that the wealthy people are happier and those who have not got so much resources as to be able to afford all the comforts and luxuries of life, cannot become happy. It is a fallacious idea. Because it is seen that rich people are more worried and more fearful as compared to those who are not so well off. Besides, because of fear and worry, they do not remain healthy, the basic need of a happy life.

When we start living and working for others, our lives become richer, more rewarding, and more meaningful. We are able to tap our inner power and strength to its highest potential. We become more energetic and creative.

Realise that selfishness is a curse to human life. Selfishness makes us narrow-minded, petty and greedy. We confine ourselves to material goals and work only for money and reward. Such a narrow vision shuts out the divine light of God from our lives. We are restricted into a groove. Our hearts and mind are contracted.

When Gandhiji was to go on the Bengal tour, two third-class compartments were reserved for him and his party. He found that two compartments were not necessary; his party could be easily accommodated only in one of them. So he called Kanu Gandhi and asked him to vacate one of the two compartments.

"But both have been reserved for us, Bapuji. The Railway authorities have been already paid," replied Kanu Gandhi.

"That does not matter at all! We are going to Bengal for the service of the poor and starving millions. It is not proper on our part to enjoy comforts on the train. Moreover, don't you observe the suffocating rush in other third-class compartments? Under such circumstances, we should not occupy more space than what is absolutely necessary. Travelling in third-class compartment with so much reserved accommodation will be a criminal joke!" observed Gandhiji.

No further arguments were necessary. The whole party moved out of one compartment, vacating it for other passengers. And then only could Gandhiji relax himself into sound sleep.

Cultivate the quality of selflessness. This is not easy at first. But as we grow in awareness, we will also grow in unselfishness. Feel your oneness with the divine spirit. Feel your oneness with all creation. Be aware of your kinship with all the creatures that breathe the breath of life. Draw inspiration from the great men who devoted their lives for the benefit of humanity.

Swami Vivekananda was once staying at the garden-house of Gopal Lal Seal in Cossipore. One day, a young man came to him and said, "Swamiji, I have visited many places and have had intimate association with many religious sects; yet I find I do not as yet understand what truth is. Every day I close the door and sit in meditation, but peace remains as elusive as ever! Swamiji tell me why?"

Swamiji patiently listened to him, then said, "My child, if you want peace, you have to do exactly the opposite of what you have been doing so long. You have to keep your door open, you have to look around. If you do, you will be surprised to find how many people are anxiously waiting for your help! Help them, feed them, give them water to drink, serve them as much as you can. I guarantee, you will get peace."

If you judge people you will have no time to love them. The world does not need any more mountains to climb or rivers to cross. What the world needs now is love, not just for some, but for everyone. If you could only love enough, you could be the most powerful person in the world. Love is the most powerful positive emotion on the earth. Love can cure, love can heal, repair, love can restore, love can reform and melt the heart of even a stone-hearted person, love can transform a sinner into a saint. That is the power of love. So let us go forth into the world with a song in our heart and a smile on our lips.

⁂

9

Have Faith in Yourself

Swami Vivekananda has said if you have faith in three million gods but have no faith in yourself your life will be doomed. It means that God helps them who help themselves. Think about Swami Vivekananda when he went to the USA to address the Parliament of Religions. He was standing in front of the great intellectuals of the world. He was in a foreign country with no acquaintances. He was in a country which was thousands of miles away from his motherland. He was in a country which had a different culture, different climate, different religion, different thinking. In fact, he was unaccustomed to everything. He had to speak in a foreign language; not only to speak but to convince them to his thinking. But Swami Vivekananda had faith in himself. He had infinite faith in his abilities. He had infinite confidence in himself and his abilities. He rose to the occasion and shook the world by his oratory skills, knowledge and clarity of thought

Whenever I am required to deliver any speech or lecture in any seminar or conference I try to remember Swami Vivekananda standing at the podium in the conference hall at the Parliament of Religions. Immediately I get charged up and my entire body and mind gets filled up with strange kind of confidence. I also advise my students to follow this method of remembering Swami Vivekananda and believe me most of them have shown remarkable improvement in their confidence and speaking power.

Just listen to the roaring words of **Swami Vivekananda**—

"Blame none for your faults. Stand upon your own feet, and take the whole responsibility upon yourself. Say, 'This misery I am suffering is of my own doing' and that very thing proves that it will have to be undone by me alone. That what I created, I can demolish'. Therefore stand up and be bold. Take the whole responsibility on your own shoulders and know that you are the creator of your own destiny. All the strength and power is within you. Therefore make your own future."

Weakness is a sure sign of death. Swami Vivekananda went to the extent of saying that weakness is a sin. Weakness brings fear and fear brings misery and death. Have faith in yourself and the almighty. Faith often works miracles. The following story highlights the power of faith.

A man wanted to cross a river. A sage gave him an amulet and said, "This will carry you across." The man, taking it in his hand, began to walk over the water. Before he had gone half the way, he was seized with curiosity, and opened the amulet to see what was in it. Therein he found, written on a piece of paper, the sacred name of Lord Rama. At this the man said depreciatingly, "Is this the whole secret?" No sooner did this scepticism enter his mind than he sank down. It is the faith which works wonders, for faith is life and want of faith is death.

Faith can achieve miracles while vanity or egotism brings about the destruction of man. The following story will make this point clear.

A disciple who had firm faith in the infinite power of his guru (spiritual teacher) walked over a river by simply uttering his name. Seeing this the guru thought, "Wo! Is there such a power in my mere name? Then how very great and powerful must I be!" The next day, the guru also tried to walk over the river uttering "I" "I", but no sooner did he step on the water than he sank and was soon drowned; for the poor man did not know how to swim even.

Abraham Lincoln said:

"You can't fail if you resolutely determine that you will not much depend on your surroundings as on your self-reliance."

We cannot possibly conquer all the objective environment. The little fish wants to fly from its enemies in water. How does it do so? By evolving wings and becoming a bird. The fish did not change the water or the air; the change was in itself. Change is always subjective. All through evolution you find that the conquest of nature comes by change in the subject. Therefore to change the world you have to change yourself. You have to belief that you are a rare gem and you can dazzle like a rare gem. To think of yourself smaller than you are is a violation of your real nature.

Washington Irving said:

"Great minds have purposes, others have wishes. Little minds are tamed and subdued by misfortune; but great minds rise above them."

Once Swami Vivekananda was having a long trek in the Himalayas when he found an old man extremely exhausted standing hopelessly at the foot of an upward slope. The man said to Swamiji in utter frustration, "Oh, sir, how to cross it; I cannot walk anymore; my chest will break."

Swamiji listened to the old man patiently and then said, "Look down at your feet. The road that is under your feet is the road that you have passed over and is the same road that you see before you; it will soon be under your feet." These words emboldened the old man and renewed his faith in himself. He resumed his onward trek and soon he reached his destination with ease.

William Blake gives us a very important thought. He says:

"Compared to what we ought to be, we are only half awake. We are making use of only a small part of our physical and mental resources."

Weak men, when they lose everything and feel themselves weak, try all sorts of uncanny methods of making money, and come to astrology and all these things. It is the coward and the fool who says, "This is fate". But it is the strong man who stands up and says, "I will make my fate". You tend to become what you think of yourself as being. Raise you appraisal of yourself.

Affirm that you have greater possibilities than have ever yet appeared. Develop your mind power. Let the whole world be at your command.

Whatever your mind can conceive and believe, it can achieve. Every advance in your life begins with an idea of some kind and since your ability to generate new ideas is unlimited, your future can be unlimited as well.

Swami Vivekananda told a very interesting story to highlight the above point. The story goes like this:

There was an astrologer who came to a king and said, "You are going to die in six months." The king was frightened out of his wits and was almost about to die then and there from fear. But his minister was a clever man, and this man told the king that these astrologers were fools. The king would not believe him. So the minister saw no other way to enable the king see that the astrologers were fools but to invite the astrologer to the palace again. There he asked him if his calculations were correct. The astrologer said that there could not be a mistake, but to satisfy him he went through the whole of the calculations again and then said that they were perfectly correct. The king's face became livid. The minister said to the astrologer, "And when do you think you will die? "In twelve years" was the reply. The minister quickly drew his sword and chopped off the astrologer's head from the body and said to the king, "Do you see this liar. He is dead this moment."

This life is a great game. Make the effort to win it. Thousands of people in this world are suffering – some have no hands, or no feet to walk with. How can you with all your faculties at your disposal, admit failure? You must not do so. When you go backward your mental outlook is so dim that you think the whole world is going backward. But you will always advance if you are accomplishing something.

A lot of people are making money and exploiting the masses in the name of astrology and fortune-telling. If people have any problem they prefer going to a 'godman' rather than to a doctor. The 'godman' blames the stars and gives amulet or rings as solution to all his problems and makes money. People have lost faith in themselves. They have forgotten that they have immense power within them to meet any challenge of life. A wonderful story told by **Shiv Khera** draws our attention to the problem of superstition and the intensity of its practice. The story goes like this—

A superstitious man believed that five was his lucky number. One day, commuting to his place of work, in a train, he noticed that his seat number was 55 and it was in the 5th coach. His ticket was numbered 555. The train arrived at platform number 5. On checking into a hotel, he was given room number 55 on the fifth floor. All this convinced him that, that day was a lucky day for him and 5 was his lucky number. So he decided to go to the races. He bet his entire savings on horse number 5. Keeping his fingers crossed he awaited the results. To his unpleasant surprise, the horse finished 5th in the race and he lost all his money.

Charles E, Merriam said:

"The future belongs to those who fuse intelligence with faith and who with courage and determination grope their way forward from chance to choice, from blind adaptation to creative evolution."

Never think lowly of yourself. You too have a divine spark inside you. Only it needs determination and commitment to make it grow into flame that will make your being resplendent with divine glory. You must shake yourself out of slumber and realise your innate greatness. Do not self-limit yourself, even in your private thoughts. Always see yourself as greater than you have ever been. Believe you can, and you will. Just remember that you always have the right to hold a high opinion of yourself.

Courage and endurance go hand in hand. One must be well prepared to suffer all sorts of indignities and even bodily pains who take up the cause of goodness and morality. The ignorant and the evil elements will do their best to restrain such a crusader from advancing further, as the history is witness to this fact.

Thomas Carlyle said:

"Obstacles in the pathway of the weak become stepping stones in the pathway of the strong."

Truth is more real than mere thought or imagination, but whatever we think or imagine may sometime come to be true. Years ago Jules Verne wrote several scientific adventure novels which at the time were regarded merely as fiction; but since then, many of his concepts have become realities.

Imagination is a very important factor in creative thought. But imagination has to ripen into conviction. You can't do that without a strong will. But if you imagine something with all the power of your will, your imagination will be converted into conviction. And when you can hold that conviction against all odds it will come true. If your will is strong, whatever you imagine will be created for you. It is a fact.

There is one thing you must never do. It is you must never, as long as you live, stop believing in yourself. You know that the elephant is a much larger animal than the lion. The elephant's body seems to be much stronger than the body of a lion, and yet a single lion can put to flight a whole herd of elephants. What is the secret of lion's power? It's faith in itself, its self reliance. The lion practically believes its power to be infinite, its inner force illimitable. The elephants would have realised that a single one of them is capable of destroying thousands of lions, only if it has faith in itself, but the poor elephants lack faith in the inner self and the consequent courage.

Do not tread the beaten path. Do not feel bound by effete customs and conventions, but with prophet-like perception transcend time and face all the challenges and guide the world into a bright future. To have courage, think of courage. We become what we think. As you think of courage, courage will fill your thoughts and displace fear. The more courageous your thinking, the greater the courage you will have.

If you think you are beaten, you are,
If you think you dare not, you don't,
If you want to win but think you can't,
It's almost certain you won't.

If you think you will lose, you are lost,
For out in the world we find,
Success begins with a person's will—
It's all in the state of mind.

If you think you are outclassed, you are,
You have got to think high to rise,
You have got to be sure of yourself before
You can ever win a prize.

Life's battles don't always go,
To the stronger or faster man,
But sooner or later the one who wins,
Is the one who thinks he can.

Thomas Merton said correctly:

"Nothing which is worth doing is ever done without great sacrifice. Every dream in its unfolding has difficult times, times when those who work with it are discouraged, when it seems as though those who were committed to it have lost the vision."

One, who has strong desire to succeed, becomes great. Those who have no desire to succeed or excel can't do anything in life. They simply fail and regret. They do not trust their abilities and give up before commencing a task. If you have a strong desire for any task and use your mental power, then you will gain success. People having faith in themselves can do anything and everything in life. No one can stop them from getting success. They are ready to risk themselves for their aim and nothing is impossible for them.

The greatest obstacle in solving problems is the belief that you cannot solve them. As **Emerson** said, **"A man is what he thinks about all the day long."** If you think of success, you create an atmosphere in which success is probable. If you think of failure, you set a stage for it. A person should pray for courage as he prays for his daily bread. And your prayer for courage will enable you to think and act with courage. The hammer shatters the glass but forges steel. Similarly, trouble may demolish your business but built your character.

Norman Vincent Peale has rightly said:

"The blow at the outward man maybe the greatest blessing to the inner man."

The condition today is that the young men and women who possess unlimited energy are unaware of their capacity and power. They do not have the necessary courage to face the challenges that come their way so that they may be able to meet them squarely with bravery and fortitude. What an irony and mockery it may appear that being rich in all faculties such young people become coward and continue to suffer the ignominy like slaves of our own people.

For thousands of years, no one believed it was possible for a human being to run a mile in less than four minutes. But on May 6, 1954, Roger Bannister proved that the impossible was possible. How did he do it? First he decided it was possible to do it, and that he could do it. He began by constantly imagining the event taking place successfully over and over again in his mind. He saw himself breaking through the four minute barrier literally hundreds and hundreds of times, creating clear, convincing depictions of himself accomplishing his goal with so much emotional intensity that his subconscious and nervous system were programmed to carry it out.

His success of course prompted others to change their own belief system. Within the next eighteen months, twenty-four other runners proceeded to break the four-minute mile. In the following decade, several hundred other accomplished the same feat. The barrier proved to be mental, not physical. This is a prime example of how thought plus faith creates form.

Listen to the inspiring voice of **Swami Vivekananda**:

"What our country now wants are muscles of iron and nerves of steel, gigantic wills which nothing can resist, which

can penetrate into the mysteries and the secrets of the universe and will accomplish their purpose in any fashion, even if it meant going down to the bottom of the ocean and meeting death face to face."

Man is the maker of his destiny. No doubt, heredity and environment play a significant role in shaping it. The component of heredity is beyond human control. But even if it is unfavourable, its negative effects can be neutralised to a certain extent through judicious rational exercise. Environment can be changed. We can create an environment congenial to us. A lighted lamp, wherever it is, creates an environment of light. Put the sandalwood anywhere, it will fill everything around it with fragrance. So like the lighted lamp or the sandalwood we can carry our environment with us.

Computer is the creation of human mind. Can you realise the performance and power of a computer? It can make complicated calculations in seconds. Just think how much powerful and intelligent is the human mind which created such computer. Yes, your brain is much more powerful than the most powerful computer of the world. Believe in your brain or mind.

It is not life that matters, but it is the courage that you bring to it. Courage is the standing army of the soul which keeps it from conquest, pillage and slavery. It is a tremendous error to feel helpless. Do not seek help from anyone. We are our own help. If we cannot help ourselves, there is none to help us. You are your only friend and you are your only enemy. Have faith in yourself. The creator has planted in each of us the capacity to deal with our problems. What, then, prevents so many people from reaching their own solutions. It is not lack of intelligence, as a rule, or lack of education. Almost always, it is because they have certain roadblocks in their minds, psychic obstacles that limit or paralyse their problem – solving abilities.

If you want something done, rather than waiting for luck to look your way, take steps to get it done. Instead of sailing through life as a passenger, become the captain of the ship, leading things in the direction you chose to move in rather than reacting to the whim of the changing tides.

As **Robin Sharma** says:

"To become more proactive during the weeks ahead, begin to see yourself as the Chief Executive officer of your destiny, the CEO of your life."

A story told by **Norman Vincent Peale** goes like this—

A tornado swept through a city in south-western US doing great damage. A mother there, confined to her bed because of infantile paralysis, paralysed from the waist down, at the height of the tornado became alarmed for her two small children in the next room. There was no one to help; the tornado was striking the house with force. Her limbs were assumed to be without power, but concern for the safety of her children was stronger than her limitations. Slowly she got out of bed and painfully made her way into the adjoining room taking her babies in her arms, she walked with them out of the house. Love proved more powerful than the paralysis from which she had been told she might never recover.

Norman Vincent Peale concludes the story by saying that some people become paralysed, not in their limbs, but in their thoughts. They accept limitations by saying, "This is all I can do".

Listen to what **Anne Frank** has said:

"Everyone has inside of him a piece of good news. The good news is that you really do not know, how great you can be, how much you can love, what you can accomplish, and what your potential is."

One definitely succeeds due to one's dedication and strong desire. All one does need is concentration of his energies at one focal point. We waste our time in worrying about useless topics and nurture doubt of various types about ourselves. These thoughts provoke our mind and disable us. Consequently, we do not have strong dedication. We become weak and lose our energy.

Too many people are leaving the quality of their futures to chance rather than to choice. We need to keep our ears and eyes open to the realities of life. If we do not act on life and take action to make things happen, it will act on us and give us results we might not want. We should remember that all it takes to change the course of history is a small group of genuinely interested citizens.

God helps those who help themselves. We must try our best by working hard and surely and certainly God will be kind to us to bestow on us the glory we deserve. We should never forget the fact – "First deserve and then desire". As a matter of fact, one needs not even desire, as success is likely to come automatically, because we have worked for it.

Thomas Edison said:

"If we did all the things we are capable of doing, we would literally astonish ourselves."

Do not make yourself cringing, sneaking, miserable creatures. As you think, so will you become. Think of yourself to be powerful and powerful you will become. Think yourself to be free and free you are this moment.

Self-doubt makes people afraid to stand up to their problems. But the truth is, when you do stand up to your difficulties, very often your difficulties will no longer stand up to you.

When a cat comes, pigeons close their eyes: they think the cat does not see them because they do not see the cat, nevertheless the cat eats them up. If you are afraid, the cat will eat you up. Have you not noticed that while walking in the suburban quarters, if we betray the least sign of fear, even dogs rush at us and molest us? Dogs even will tear us if we fear. But if we are fearless, we can overcome and tame lions and tigers.

Swami Vivekananda said:

"If you want true success, choose an ideal. Think about it, dream about it and follow it. Remove all other thoughts and concentrate on it. You would definitely succeed. You will have to go deep to bring the pearls of success. One must not lose heart against adverse circumstances to continuously progress in life."

We should not think about fate or depend on it. Sometimes it is dangerous to know our fate. This is because if someone knows about his good luck, he would not work hard and become lazy. He would expect results without hard work. One, who knows about one's bad luck, would be disappointed. One would not work hard because one would know beforehand that he or she is not going to receive anything, howsoever hard he might work. So, it is not in one's favour to know one's fate. It poses hindrance to work.

**

10

The Power of Prayer

A few days back, my younger son who is just two years old fell from a height and seriously hurt his head. Soon after the fall he became very quiet and started feeling drowsy. After about half an hour he vomited. He was taken to doctor and the doctor said that the symptoms indicate brain haemorrhage or internal injury of the brain. He said it was a serious condition and advised immediate hospitalisation for checkup.

My sixth sense indicated that there was not enough time for medical interference and taking him to hospital would be futile because there was not much time to go through all this. I felt that prayer to my God, 'Baba' was the only hope. I got down on my knees and surrendered myself completely to him. I said "Baba, my son's life is in your hands. Save him 'Baba'. I prayed to my 'Baba' with total faith, honesty and sincerity for saving the life of my child and as I prayed tears rolled down my cheeks. Suddenly, I heard the soft voice of 'Baba' saying, "Don't worry, it was indeed a serious injury. The clot was forming in the brain but I am dissolving the clot and the injury will be healed." As soon as I heard this voice I was relieved. My parents were getting ready to take him to hospital. I told them that it was no longer required as I have got the message of 'Baba' and he will be alright. Within a few minutes my son became normal and cheerful and started playing as before. He smiled, laughed and jumped as if nothing had happened. Tears once again rolled down my cheeks as I looked at the smiling face of my son and then the image of 'Baba'. I had realised the miracle of prayer, the power of faith and the love of my 'Baba'.

That day I was confirmed of one thing – "True, sincere and honest prayers are always answered". What is required is complete faith and total surrender at the holy feet of almighty. There should not be any trace of doubt or else everything will come to nought. Just as a small hole in the pot can drain away all the water from the pot, in the same way a little doubt in God can drain away the power of faith and prayer.

The most powerful energy anyone can generate is prayer-energy. God is never more than a prayer away from you. Let you heart pant for him as a miser longs for gold and money. As the drowning man pants hard for breath, so must one's heart yearn for the Lord.

Mahatma Gandhi was right when he said:

"It is the faith that steers us through stormy seas, faith that moves mountains and faith that jumps across ocean. That faith is nothing but living wide-awake consciousness of God within. He who has achieved that faith wants nothing."

In prayer, whatever the creed or denomination, one accepts the concept of the creator who is the source of life and to whom one can turn in humility and trust. The attitude that "Not my will but thine be done" can produce astonishing results. Whether you choose to call it mobilising the unconscious or making contact with God, prayer is a channel through which enormous power can flow.

If you must be mad, be it not for the temporary things of the world. Be mad for the love of God. Some men shed streams of tears because sons are not born to them; others eat away their hearts in sorrow because they cannot get riches. But alas! How many are there who weep for not having seen the Lord. There are very few people indeed who seek the Lord, weep for him, and really pray to him.

We spend hours together watching TV, cinema, etc. Yet nobody has leisure to think of the glory of the almighty God even for twenty-four minutes out of the twenty-four hours of the day.

When your prayer or wishes are not successful, it is because you have no will, no faith on the power of God. If with a doubting mind you ask God to heal you, you won't be healed.

John Mason has rightly said:

"When you feel swept off your feet, get back to your knees."

Time spent in communion with God is never lost. The highest purpose of faith or prayer is not to change my circumstances but to change me. Pray to do the will of God in every situation – nothing else is worth praying for. Prayer may not change all things for you, but it surely changes you for all things. Whenever you feel restless sit down for prayer and your restlessness will simply vanish.

Prayer is the medium through which we express our inner feelings, with firm faith in God. Just as we ring up our friend and communicate an urgent message, so do we communicate with God through prayer and bare our heart. It is a sacred dialogue with God. Prayer is direct speaking to God.

Mahatma Gandhi beautifully describes the purpose of prayer in the following golden words:

"The purpose of prayer is to awaken the divinity in the depth of our heart. He who has realised the efficacy of prayer can live for days together without food. But without prayer he cannot live even for a moment. Prayer is the breath of life."

Man's need for prayer is as great as his need for bread. As food is necessary for the body, prayer is necessary for the soul. True prayer never goes unanswered. When the mind is full of prayerful thought, everything in the world seems good and agreeable. Prayer is essential for progress of life.

Dr. Alexis Carrel said:

"Prayer is the most powerful form of energy one can generate, it is as real as terrestrial gravity. Prayer, like radium, is a source of luminous, self-generating energy.... In prayer, human beings seek to augment their finite energy by addressing themselves to the infinite source of all energy. When we pray, we link ourselves

with the inexhaustible motive power that spins the universe. We pray that a part of this power be apportioned, to our needs. Even in asking, our human deficiencies are filled, and we arise strengthened and repaired.... When we address God in fervent prayer, we change both soul and body for the better."

Once upon a time conceit entered into the heart of a pious person and he thought that there was no greater devotee than himself. Reading his heart, the Lord said to the man,

"Go to such and such a place, a great devotee of mine is living there. Cultivate his acquaintance; for he is truly devoted to me." The man went there and found a farmer, who rose early in the morning, prayed to God only once and taking his plough went out and tilled the ground all day long. At night, he went to bed after praying to God once more. The man said to himself, "How can this rustic be a lover of God? I see him busily engaged in worldly duties and he has no signs of a pious man about him."

The man went back to the Lord and spoke what he thought of his new acquaintance. Thereupon the Lord said to the man, "Take this cup of oil and go round this city and come back with it. But take care that you do not spill even a single drop of oil." The man did as he was told and on his return the Lord asked him, "Well how many times did you remember me and my name in the course of your walk round the city?" "Not once, my Lord," said the man, "and how could I when I had to watch this cup brimming over with oil?"

The Lord then said, "This one cup of oil did so divert your attention that even you forgot me altogether. But look at that rustic (farmer), who though carrying the heavy burden of a family, still remembers me twice everyday."

According to **Charles Spurgeon,**

"Prayer time is never wasted time. Sometimes we think we are too busy to pray. That is a great mistake, for praying is a savings of time."

When you take one step toward God, He will take more steps toward you than you could ever count. Prayer alone proves that you trust God. When mind and speech unite earnestly asking for a thing, that prayer is answered. Of no avail are the prayers of that man who says with his mouth— "These are all thine, O Lord", and at the same time thinks in his heart that all of them are his.

Pray for more and more faith. He who has faith gets everything. For, as the wonderful proverb tells us, faith can indeed move mountains. The Bible also tells us the same thing: "Everything is possible to him who believeth." Therefore, pray for faith as a famished person prays for food, and a thirsty person for water. Accept God's plan for you, and surrender to the Divine Will. It is to feel sure that whatever God does is always for the best. It is to grow in the realisation that, when God seems to deny you, His own child, He denies some good thing that you do desire, but He designs to give you something better than your desired thing.

Prayer is not mere lip service. It is not a matter of uttering articulated, good words. It is not a well-evaluated bargaining or calculation. It is what springs out with utmost faith in the power of God.

Swami Jagadatmananda says:

"Prayer supplements and complements meditation. With the help of intense prayer meditation becomes easy. Before starting meditation it is better to pray for ten or fifteen minutes with a concentrated mind. Just as with the gathering of clouds, there will be a break of showers, when the prayer becomes intense, the mind rises, goes beyond the level of emotional heart and reaches the spiritual heart. The eyes brim with tears. This is the beginning of intense yearning for God. Here is the fulfilment of meditation."

The knot of life's hardships is not easy to untie. It is only by prayer that this knot can gradually melt. This is the real power of prayer. Prayer is the spiritual solution of seeking peace.

I agree with **John Mason's** comments – **"Do deep praying before you find yourself in a deep hole."**

A man was watering a sugarcane field throughout the day. After finishing his task he found that not a drop of water had entered the field. All the water had run underground through several big rat-holes. Such is the state of the man who prays God, secretly cherishing ambitions and worldly desires in his heart. Though he may be praying daily he makes no progress because his entire devotion runs to waste through the rat-holes of these desires and at the end of his lifelong devotion and prayer he remains the same as before.

Brooks Phillips laid down the golden rule for praying. He said:

"I do not pray for a lighter load but for a stronger back."

One thing I have realised as clear as daylight that it is impossible to be prayerful and pessimistic at the same time. Being prayerful and pessimistic is contradictory to each other and cannot co-exist. Prayer makes you optimistic and makes you confident of your abilities. It makes you feel that you are not alone in this world. There is somewhere your friend, philosopher and guide watching your every step and ready to help you whenever you need Him.

Sri Ramkrishna used to say:

"God can hear the footsteps of even an ant. Won't he then hear your prayer? When your yearning is ripe, He is sure to hear your voice."

Let prayer become a habit with you. Pray, pray and continue to pray. So many of our prayers are unanswered, because we give up praying. We become impatient and lose faith. We feel that as God is not going to act for us. What we forget is that God acts at the right time. If He has not yet acted, it only means that the right time has not come yet. This applies not only to our material requirements, but also to our mental and spiritual needs.

Prayer makes you move on the right path. It helps you from deviating from your principles and your mission. It protects you from the temptation of the world which appears sweet and delicious at the beginning but in long run they ruin the person completely.

The nearer you are to God through prayer, the less you will have occasions to cry or weep. The further we are from Him, the more will long faces come. The more we know of Him through prayer, the more misery vanishes.

We will be losers if we do not trust or pray to God. God won't lose anything if we threaten him saying, "I won't believe in you if you don't make my life absolutely smooth, absolutely free from all worries and problems." We must pray to God sincerely with self-surrender and devotion. Certainly it will do us immense good.

Author **O. Hallesby** says:

"Begin to realise more and more that prayer is the most important thing you do. You can use your time to no better advantage than to pray whenever you have an opportunity to do so, either alone or with others; while at work or while at rest, anywhere."

Man prays God not only for that God might remember him, but also that he should remember God. We derive maximum power from prayer when we use it not as a petition but as a supplication that we may become more like him. Regular prayer paves the way for physical well-being. It opens up the fountain of energy and confidence in people. They get inspired in turn to instil this spirit of enthusiasm and energy in others.

A man often builds castles in the air, sees dreams of perfection, when he is young, physically strong, and when he is endowed with a sense of confidence. But with the waves of failure, diffidence, resistance from others, a sense of inadequacy and helplessness shakes him off his ground. When he is struck by these problems, he can neither think nor consult others and seek relief from anxiety. In these situations we can find solace in prayer.

According to **Dwight L. Moody**,

"Spread out your petition before God and then say, thy will not mine be done. The sweetest lesson I have learned in God's school is to let the Lord choose for me."

The daily practice of silence, prayer and meditation are the most effective techniques for making the mind healthy, stable and focused. Do not wait for bitter experiences, serious reversals of fortune and major illnesses to afflict you before you turn to God. Turn to Him in your period of prosperity and peace: put him first in your life always.

Barendra Kumar brings out the true nature of prayer. He says:

"Prayer is communication with God – expressing thankfulness or asking blessings. It is a welcome to God to enter in you. It is a supplication to fulfil your aim, your ambition, your goal. It is an effort to seek advice. It is an attempt to get comfort in times of trouble. It is commitment to follow him. It is the method to purify the outer and the inner. It is way to be controlled, to be guided, to be led. It is a pledge to live under his grace. It is a quest – to know the purpose of life and to achieve a higher end with his power."

Let me repeat these words once again – *Do not wait for bitter experiences, serious reversals of fortune and major illnesses to afflict you before you decide to turn to God. Turn to Him in your period of prosperity and peace: put Him first in your life always.*

Listen to what **E.M Bounds** says on the power of prayer – **"Prayer is our most formidable weapon; the thing which makes all else we do efficient."**

There is only one permanent solution to all sorrows and sufferings. That is to surrender ourselves at the feet of the Lord. Every mother is moved by the children crying in pain. Mother is by nature kind. God is like mother. Let us continue to pray and repeat the name of God. Let us cry for Him and then like a loving mother He will take us in His arms and make you free.

Constant prayer is the only way to get freedom from anxiety. God knows about each devotee's needs. Prayers can effect transformation. If sorrow overpowers you, offer your prayers in whatever manner you like. Continue your tearful prayers to God with added vigour and spirit. You may not feel the efficacy of the prayer at once, but in the long run it is sure to help you.

Listen to what **Alexis Carrel** says about prayer—

"If you make a habit of sincere prayer, your life will be very noticeably and profoundly altered. Prayer stamps with its indelible mark our actions and demeanour. A tranquility of bearing, a facial and bodily repose are observed in those whose inner lives are thus enriched. Within the depths of consciousness a flame kindles. And man sees himself. He discovers his selfishness, his silly pride, his fears, his greeds, his blunder. He develops a sense of moral obligation, intellectual humility. Thus begins a journey of the soul toward the realm of grace."

Never miss your daily appointment with God. You deceive yourself when you are too busy, too involved in your work to find time for God. We are taxing our minds and hearts with so much useless activities that too need to be charged, recharged by contact with the greatest of all power-sources – God.

Once an elderly gentleman visited Sri Ramakrishna. He had lost his faith in God. He told Sri Ramakrishna, "I am now fifty-five and for the last fourteen years I have been in quest of God. I have faithfully followed the advice of my guru: I have been on pilgrimage, I have met innumerable holy men, but I have gained nothing. Instead I have lost my peace of mind. I have tried my best but now I am not able to pray to God. Do I have any more hope?"

Sri Ramkrishna smiled and told him, "Can you pray this much, with all sincerity and earnestness, 'Oh my God, if you really exist, then please make yourself known to me and remove my agony.' Have faith and continue your prayers. Don't crave for immediate results. You shall succeed."

The man decided to put the words of Sri Ramakrishna to test. A year later he met him. Prostrating before him he said sobbing, "Oh my master, you saved me, you showed me the path." Now he had been relieved of his depression and he had regained his faith in God.

Norman Vincent Peale says:

"If you live with God as a friend, he will become so real that He will be your sturdy companion day and night. The

sense of God's presence steadies us, gives us an anchor in the storm, and provides a reservoir of personal power. Then, even when the going is difficult, your heart can be happy within, for you have Him with you."

Let us resolve, right away to live and work for the love of God, and for that alone. We do not know how many days yet remain to us. We may be called away any time. We live in a world of uncertainty; we live the kind of life in which the only certainty is that we shall all die one day. Human life is like a volcano which may erupt any time. Therefore, let us devote our life to God. Whatever we do let us do it for the love of God.

In the **Bhagavad Gita,** Lord Krishna says:

"Fix your mind on Me; be devoted to Me; worship Me; bow down to Me. Thus having controlled thyself, and making Me thy goal supreme, thou shalt come unto Me."

Can there be a greater assurance than this? Can there be a better option for struggling human souls. By giving our whole heart to God, by living and adoring Him, by worshipping Him always, we will find Him – the Lord of our life and destiny.

The Almighty has assured all of us in the **Holy Koran**:

"I reside in the hearts of those who intensely yearn for me."

The Bible says:

"Ask, and it shall be given unto you; seek and ye shall find; knock, it shall be opened unto you."

If we carefully observe we shall find that there is no difference in the essence of all the three religions – Hinduism, Islam and Christianity. It is surprising fact that religion continues to be a major source of conflict, hatred, violence and war and we continue fighting with each other in the name of religion without understanding the essence of our religion.

**

11

Come Out of Your Narrow Well

One day while I was lecturing in a class, the topic of discussion shifted to Margaret Thatcher, the former Prime Minister of England. I told the students that Margaret Thatcher was a very 'handsome' lady. As soon as I had said this, a student named Pintu stood up and said, "Sir the word 'handsome' is used in case of masculine gender but you used it in respect of a lady. Sir you made a major error." I knew that Pintu was living in his narrow well and it was useless to argue with him at that moment of time. I was sure that without any documentary evidence it would be very difficult to convince him that, the word 'handsome' can be used in respect of women also. So at that moment I just said, "Thank you for correcting me but I feel that I am not incorrect." Next day, I brought all the advanced dictionaries including Cambridge and Oxford dictionaries where it was clearly mentioned that the word 'handsome' can be used to describe powerful and beautiful women.

Pintu felt quite ashamed and embarrassed and asked forgiveness for his behaviour the previous day. I said, "Pintu, it is not your fault. Actually you are living in a narrow well and have confined yourself within that well. You have to expand yourself. You have to know that there are bigger wells than the well that you own and only then you will be able to develop yourself. You have to view everything with an open mind. If you confine yourself within your narrow well you will become stagnant and ultimately you will suffocate yourself. You have to see and appreciate others' point of view. Only then, there will be progress and development."

At this very moment I am reminded of a story told by Swami Vivekananda at The Parliament of Religions at Chicago. The story went like this—

A frog lived in a well. It had lived there for a long time. It was born and brought up there. One day another frog that lived in the sea came and fell into the well. "Where are you from," asked the frog of the well.

"I am from the sea," answered the frog from the sea.

"The sea! How big is that? Is it as big as my well?" the frog said and took a leap from one side of the well to the other.

"My friend" said the frog from the sea. "how do you compare the sea with your little well?"

Then the frog took another leap and asked, "Is your sea so big?"

"What nonsense you speak, to compare the sea with your well!"

"Well then," said the frog of the well, "nothing can be bigger than my well; there can be nothing bigger than this; this fellow is a liar, so turn him out."

We are all sitting in our own well. We think that the whole world is our little well. This is the reason for all this variance and dispute. Let us come out of our wells and see the vast sea. Only then we shall realise how much beautiful the world looks.

Let us cast away our ego in the filthiest gutter of the world. Ego is the root cause of all problems. An egoist is a fool but considers himself wise, and when anyone tries to obstruct him, he becomes violent. An egoist sits in his narrow well and considers himself the greatest and all-knowing. He never considers anyone better than him. The moment you sacrifice your ego, your qualities start emerging from your inside and it leads to spiritualism. You become more forgiving and benevolent. The problem is that sitting for a long time in one's little well makes it a comfort zone and then it becomes very difficult for the person to come out of that comfort zone. The result is that his growth and development is stagnated and he dies with music still in him.

For example, if you are placed in an uncomfortable situation such as public speaking, stress can turn on, resulting in your trying to avoid the situation and to get back to your non-public speaking comfort zone. This is because you don't consciously seek discomfort and you would rather get back to the comfortable way of doing things. This usually happens when you want to bring in change or try to be different from your normal self, change habit patterns and use new skills, etc., but if you stick with the new and sustain the change despite the early discomfort you get used to it and your comfort zone expands. "Stick with it" is the key.

Move outside your comfort zone or your narrow well and find adventure, excitement and new levels of satisfaction. Stretch your comfort zones by trying something new.

Dr. Harikrishna Devsare tells us a beautiful story to highlight how ego makes a person blind to the good qualities of other person. The story goes like this—

One day, a gold coin was found near useless papers. The coin laughed at papers and said, "O dirty papers, get away. I am feeling unpleasant. Don't you know I am gold coin? Everyone is crazy about me."

That heap of paper sheets was taken to a paper mill and there, it was turned into currency notes. When the currency notes were ready, each currency note was equivalent to ten coins. When the notes were being counted, the gold coin was present there coincidentally. The paper (currency) said, "Listen, ego is not virtue. You were criticising me that day and I am ten times more powerful than you today. So never consider anyone worthless."

I remember the day when I first came out of my narrow well and believe me, dear friends it was a wonderful feeling. I felt so light and free. I was pursuing my graduation at that time. One day, the son of my neighbour came to me for some suggestion for writing an essay. As I was dictating to him some points I noticed that he had misspelt the word 'definition'. Actually he had written it correctly but till that day I believed that the spelling of the word "Definition" was "Defination". I rebuked the boy and said, "You don't know this simple spelling. You will never pass in your examination." He was a little confused but said, "I think what I have written is absolutely correct; I have no doubt that you are wrong in this matter." I was a little bit ruffled by his behaviour. I said, "I am surprised by your arrogance. You better change your behaviour or else you will be in problem." Saying this, I asked him to go home.

I went home and just to confirm myself I opened a dictionary and checked the spelling of the word 'definition'. To my surprise I found that the student was correct. I felt guilty and sorry for the boy. I did not wait for the next morning to say sorry to the boy. I immediately went to his house and apologised for my mistake. I also thanked the boy for correcting me and teaching me a very important lesson of life. That very moment I had come out of my narrow well and experienced an immense joy – joy of expansion.

Carani N Rao tells us about the paradox of our time in these beautiful words—

We have taller buildings, but shorter tempers;

We have wider freeways, but narrower viewpoints;

We spend more, but have less;

We buy more, but enjoy less;

We have multiplied possessions, but reduced our values;

We talk too much, love seldom and hate too often,

We have added years to life, but not life to years;

We have been all the way to the moon and back, but have trouble crossing the street to meet the new neighbour,

We have conquered outer space, but not the inner space;

We have cleaned up the air, but polluted the soul;

We have slit the atom, but not our prejudice;

We have higher incomes, but lower morals;

We have become long on quantity, but short on quality;
These are the times of tall men and short character;
Steep profits and shallow relationships.

Once, Swami Vivekananda was on his way to Vrindavan from Agra. As he reached the outskirts of the town he saw a man contently smoking tobacco by the wayside. Swamiji was tired as he had walked a long way. He felt an urge to smoke and take some rest. So he approached the man and asked him if he could smoke his 'Hookah' (Pipe). The very proposal made the man shudder. He said to Swamiji, "I am sorry, sir! I cannot allow you to smoke this pipe which I have used. You are a monk while I am a sweeper belonging to a low caste."

Swamiji said nothing and resumed his walk. But having gone some distance, it struck him in a flash – "What! Am I not a 'sanyasi' who has renounced everything including the idea of caste, family prestige and so forth? What a shame that I would not smoke his pipe only because he is low caste sweeper." The thought made him so restless that he at once came back to the man and made him prepare the pipe and then he joyfully smoked the pipe.

Like Swamiji let us all come out of our narrow well and embrace everybody without the distinction of caste, religion, creed, and so on. Then we shall get real happiness and real bliss. The whole world will seem to be your family and feelings like jealousy and hatred will just vanish in the thin air.

If you come out of your narrow well you will become more innovative and imaginative. Always try to generate new ideas. This mind is storehouses of infinite ideas. The problem is that we are attached to laziness that we do not try to tax the mind for finding out new ideas

I remember a story which clearly shows what innovative ideas can do to your life. The story goes as follows:

There was a wise king who had three sons. He wanted the wisest and the ablest among them to be the next king. So he decided to test his three sons. He told each one of them to fill the old palace with something and gave them one gold coin each. The first son thought that his father

had gone mad. How could he fill the whole palace with something with such a small amount? So he squandered the money on booze.

The second son thought that garbage was the cheapest thing available for the given amount, so he filled the palace with garbage.

The third son pondered over and applied his mind and came out with an innovative idea. He bought and lighted candles and incense sticks and filled the whole palace with light and fragrance.

Read this interesting story:

An Indian farmer died leaving behind 17 cows for his three sons. The will advised the eldest to take one-half, the middle one to take one-third and the youngest to take one-ninth. Since there were 17 cows, they were having problems in dividing.

One day, a wise man heard about this dispute. He decided to come with his cow and do what was needed. The wise man added his cow to the 17 making it 18. The eldest landed up getting one-half or 9 cows, the second, one-third or 6 cows and the youngest one-ninth or 2 cows. Having given away 9+6+2=17 cows, he walked away with his cow. He had done what was necessary by innovative thinking.

Some years back I used to take classes in the first year LL.B in Hooghly Mohsin Government College. One day, I was teaching my favourite subject, Jurisprudence. I was discussing Austin's Analytical theory with great enthusiasm. Suddenly a boy named Mohit got up and said,

"Sir I think you are wrong on this particular point."

I was a bit surprised by his remark. But I liked and appreciated the confidence of the boy. A student challenging a teacher on his favourite subject is not a common sight. I tried to explain my point once again as I had a feeling that he had misunderstood my previous explanation. But Mohit was not convinced and he still maintained that I was wrong and he could prove it. The other students asked Mohit to cool down and some of them rebuked him for his arrogance. As the period was almost over I told Mohit that I shall consult the books once again on that particular point and also asked him to do the same and assured him that we shall continue our discussions tomorrow. The problem was that Mohit had only a limited knowledge of the subject and he was not able to see the point in its entirety. He was not at that time prepared to come out of his narrow well.

Next day, as I was sitting in the staff room, Mohit came to me and with his head down and eyes looking at the floor said,

"Sir, I went through the books yesterday night and realised my mistake. You were absolutely right sir. I am sorry for my behaviour in the class yesterday."

I was happy that Mohit had realised his error and just patted him at the back. That very moment Mohit started sobbing uncontrollably like a child. I asked him what the matter was. He said in choking voice,

"Sir, actually I thought that you will scold me for my behaviour yesterday and rebuke me for my arrogance and rudeness but you did not say anything. Your silence and your love towards me even after such behaviour on my part made me emotional."

Mohit is now a successful lawyer and whenever we meet he reminds me of the above incident and we become nostalgic.

**

12

Learn to Forgive

One day as I was reading a book on forgiveness, I felt an irritation on my hand. I saw a mosquito sitting on my hand, sucking my blood. My first reaction was to smash it by my right palm, but something inside me prevented me from executing my desire. I questioned myself whether it was justified to award death sentence to a living being just for sucking one-thousand part of a 'drop' of blood from my body. I reasoned. Should I kill a living being only because it is satisfying its hunger on which it has no control? I felt how easy it was to smash the tiny creature with a little effort of my palm, but how difficult it was to restrain oneself from killing it and forgiving it. How much mental power and strength it requires to forgive a person who has wronged you and how much happiness you get after forgive that person.

I suddenly felt happy for not killing the mosquito. I started enjoying watching the mosquito feeding on my blood. I felt that at least I have been able to feed one tiny living being. I learnt a new lesson on forgiveness. What books were not able to teach me, this little mosquito taught me that day. That day I realised the power and miracle of forgiveness. It remains till today one of my greatest realisations. That is the reason I have included a chapter on forgiveness in this book.

I had conducted a survey with about 100 students by asking them a simple question. The question was – "If you suddenly come to know that you have only 15 minutes left to live what would you do?" About 90 percent of the students said that they would like to seek forgiveness for their sins from God and everybody to whom they had wronged and also to forgive those who had wronged them. This is the miracle of forgiveness. It heals our very souls.

I still get tears in my eyes when I imagine Lord Jesus being crucified by his executioners and even at that moment of so much pain and agony his soft sweet words – "Father forgive them for they know not what they do". How much strength, how much power is required to speak these words. After so much of sufferings at the hands of his executioners, Jesus still cared about these people. he still loved them, he still wanted their well-being. He still felt that it is not their fault because they are ignorant; they are ignorant like a child or a mad person. He knew that God would not forgive his executioners for their heinous crime, therefore he prayed to his father for them. Oh! Beautiful are these words. If all the religious books are lost, these lines will be enough to guide people for million and million of years, because the essence of all the religious teachings is present in these words of Lord Jesus.

If you have an impulse to simply forgive someone do not ignore it. Do not dismiss it, and do not postpone it. There is no revenge as sweet as forgiveness. The only people you should try to get even with are those who have helped you. Forgiveness heals, while unforgiveness wounds. When we think about offences, trouble grows; when we forgive, trouble goes.

Joseph Joubert said: **"Never cut what can be untied."**

Forgiveness acts as soothing balm for your burning heart and makes you immediately light and free. It does not matter whether other person deserves forgiveness or not, but at least you deserve your peace of mind.

According to **Shiv Khera,**

"The concept of asking for forgiveness and forgiving applies to those whose conscience is not dead. Life is too short to carry on with grudges. Negative feelings like guilt, revenge and anger are detrimental to our daily living. They are prime causes of stress and result in physical and emotional problems. They are like excess baggage that a person carries with him. If a person, who has made a mistake, be it honest or deliberate, apologises, his

heart feels light. The one who forgives feels light as well because he has let go of a grudge. Grudges have a negative cumulative effect and they bring down the energy levels of a person."

Let us listen to what **Auriela Mccarthy** has to say on this point:

"The only reason to forgive is to set yourself free of your past so you can step into the myriad of available futures that you can't see through the eyes of pain. Forgiveness swings open the door to the power of God and delivers you to the other side."

Real forgiveness involves no holding back at all. One must go the whole distance in restoring relationships. If one says, "I will forgive you for the wrong you have done to me, but I can never forget it", that is qualified forgiveness. To make it real forgiveness forgetting must be added.

H.C. Mattern gave us a beautiful formula for happiness. The formula indirectly has a special place for love and forgiveness. He said:

"Keep your heart free from hate, your mind free from worry. Live simply, expect little, give much. Fill your life with love, scatter sunshine. Forget self, think of other. Do as you would be done by. Try this for a week and you will be surprised."

It has been rightly said by **Er M.K Gupta**:

"Forgiveness is mainly for releasing yourself from negative feelings and mental unrest. It does not mean that the person concerned has escaped the results of his wrong actions. There is cosmic justice which does not spare anybody and takes care of everything. But we need not break our head over it."

Forgiveness comes from the realm of miraculous. It is a magic that cannot be put into the words of our language. It defies logic. It is beyond our intellectual understanding. Forgiveness is a gift. Once we experience it, once we are touched by it, its grace changes us forever.

Norman Vincent Peale says:

"The world needs millions of acts of forgiveness and repentance to flush out hate, resentment and bitterness."

The entire world looks yellow to the jaundiced eye. Therefore, remove from your heart all the hostilities. Replace it with love and joy. Turn your jaundiced eye into a loving and joyful eye, capable of seeing the love and joy that were always there. The burden of hatred and malice which you carry with you by not forgiving someone harms you much more than the person who has harmed you. Someone wrongs you or wounds you; in harbouring a feeling of revenge, you re-feel the injury and re-hurt yourself. The Hebrew Talmud says that a person who bears grudge is "like one who having cut one hand while handling a knife, avenges himself by stabbing the other hand".

Who could have said it better than **H.E Fosdick**. He says:

"Hating people is like burning down your house to get rid of a rat."

Many people die of 'grudgitis'. It is a disease which afflicts a person who bears grudge for a long time. It is healthy to get rid of grudges. They seldom hurt the other person but they can make the holder sick. Doctors say that ill-will and grudges make people sick. Forgiveness will do more towards getting them well than many pills.

Larry Bielat says: **"He who cannot forgive destroys the bridge over which he may one day need to pass."**

Unforgiveness is a terrible disease that attacks you, not the person you are mad at. Forgiveness allows your body to turn down the manufacture of those chemicals which tear you apart, body and soul. Forgiveness of others is a gift to ourselves, a healing medicine for many of our physical and emotional ills.

Auriela Mccarthy said:

"As long as there are people in our past we have not forgiven, we are not free from them. They are with us at all times, forever close, breathing down our necks, whispering into our ears, mocking us, threatening our peace of mind, a constant conscious or unconscious reminder of our pain."

There can be no greater example of forgiveness than Jesus. Think of him – betrayed by his own disciples, denied by his followers, subjected to an arbitrary, unjust trial, abandoned to the mercy of those who were determined to destroy him, condemned to be crucified alongside common criminals, reviled and ridiculed by his enemies, cruelly crowned with thorns, and finally nailed to the cross to die a terrible, painful death, and he died with those immortal words which teach all of us the cardinal virtue of forgiveness – "Forgive them, Lord, for they know not what they do".

Arnold Fox gives us a very valuable suggestion. He says:

"Have you any unfinished business? Finish it. Finish it now. Finish your business by telling those you love that you love them, those you appreciate that you appreciate them, those you respect that you respect them. Finish your business by telling everyone you feel it's necessary to tell, that you immediately and unconditionally forgive them. And be sure to tell yourself while you are at it."

The fire which you light for your enemy burns you more than him. Therefore, we hurt ourselves the most by anger and unforgiving nature.

Norman Vincent Peale made a very valid point when he said:

"People often kill their happiness and their success in life by their tongues. They explode, say a mean thing, write a sharp letter and the evil is done. And sadly, the real victim is not the other person but oneself."

Who are we to judge the actions of others? We ourselves are full of imperfections and still we are arrogant enough to say that, "I will not forgive you", or "You do not deserve my forgiveness". Just imagine if God were to have the same attitude towards us than what will be our fate. We commit mistakes and sins every day and then turn to God for forgiveness and we expect him to forgive us. Then why not forgive a person who has committed wrong against you. If you are not ready to forgive a person who has wronged you then also do not expect God to forgive you when you commit a wrong against the Divine Law.

**

13

Have a Mission in Life

If in a race, the competitors are asked to run without the finishing line, would anybody get the motivation or enthusiasm to run the race? The answer is big "NO" because there is no target or mission or goal. We all need a goal or mission in life. Without a goal or mission, life is not worth living. It will drift meaninglessly just like a rudderless boat. It will keep floating and going without reaching any destination. Then one day death will come and everything will be finished. You will die like a dog on a street ignorant and unprepared to meet the new world.

Most of us are really doing nothing in life. We say 'Nothing' is impossible. But in reality we find most of us doing 'Nothing'. 'Nothing' is therefore very much possible. When I ask the newcomers in the first year class what do they want to become in life, most of them say they are not sure or they have not yet decided. How tragic is that they are just drifting like a leaf drifting in a stream of water, wasting their valuable time in meaningless works and then one day they find that the life is all over.

Before you start out, you decide where you want to go. Would you sit in a train or bus without knowing where it was going? Obviously no. Then why do people go through life without having any destination or goal? So, you should know your destination before you start out.

Martin Luther King said:

"Every person must have a concern for self and feel a responsibility to discover his mission in life. God has given

each normal person a capacity to achieve some end. True, some are endowed with more talent than others, but God has left none of us talentless. Potential powers of creativity are within us and we have the duty to work assiduously to discover the power."

In the world a vast majority of persons are groping through this dark life without any mission or ideal at all. If a man with a mission in life makes a thousand mistakes, a man without any mission or an ideal makes fifty thousand mistakes. Think about the mission or goal of your life each and every moment. Let it enter your veins and arteries and every cells of your brain. Let your mission or ideal tingle in every drop of your blood. Let every cell of your brain play the melody of your mission. Become mad to reach your goal. Just as a lover thinks about his sweetheart all the time, keep thinking about the goal and the ways of reaching it all the time.

You should have a clear and positive goal to succeed in life. One should have the will power to achieve it and passion to accomplish it. Aimless people are like a ship without direction.

Definitiveness of purpose is the starting point of any achievement. You can have anything you want in life if you can first decide exactly what it is, and then do things accordingly to achieve the desired result.

Earl Nightingale said:

"Success does not necessarily mean that we must earn a great deal of money and live in the biggest house in the town. It only means that we are engaged in striving towards a goal that we have independently chosen, and feel it is worthy of us as persons. A goal, whatever it may be, is what gives meaning to our existence."

Selecting a steady stream of compelling goals will liberate the fullness of your talents. Make certain that your goals are worthy of you. Make sure they are the kind of challenges that will force you to reach into your heart and bring out the best within you. In order to truly manifest your human potential and leave a legacy that lasts, you must keep raising the bar and holding yourself to a higher standard. The reason for failure in life is lack of strong desire. You might have seen unsuccessful people blaming others. People often talk of unavailability of resources, lack of opportunities, etc. Those, who are unsuccessful even after being healthy, talented and stable, lack strong desire, goal and dedication in their life. Even a handicapped person can climb a mountain with extreme dedication and mission.

One must know precisely where one wants to go. Always visualise your goal in the mind. In this way your focus will always be on your goal and you won't get distracted from it.

According to **Swet Marden,**

"Those, who believed in themselves, are known in the annals of history. They knew their dream is going to become reality. Through continuous progress towards their goal, they got their names recorded in history. The world sets aside to clear the path for those who know their destination."

It is also important that one goal at a time should be pursued or else the consequence will be like the priest in the following story—

There were two brothers. One was a priest and the other was a farmer. One day, the farmer went to see his priest brother at his residence. A servant in the house said, "My master is busy. He is praying to Lord Shiva."

The farmer said that he would wait outside and came out of the house. The farmer went out and started digging a pit.

After sometime, when the farmer enquired, the servant replied,"My master is still busy. Now he is praying to Lord Vishnu."

The farmer started digging a second pit. Again after sometime, when the farmer asked, the servant said that now his master was praying to Goddess Kali. The farmer dug yet another pit.

This continued. Every time the servant announced that his master was praying to some God, the farmer dug a new pit.

At last the priest finished his prayers and came out. The farmer rose and went to see him. The priest noticed the pits on the riverbed and asked him,"What for did you dig so many pits?"

"For water," replied the farmer.

The priest laughed and said, "You fool! You could have got water by now had you dug only one pit deep enough."

"You fool! You could have got salvation by now had you prayed to only one God instead of many," replied the farmer brother.

The man with limited intuition and with a mind of lower order does not take the slightest trouble to pursue wisdom owing to his fear of the difficulties with which he may meet; and, if he does make an attempt, he stops as soon as he encounters an obstacle. On the other hand, the man of superior mind never ceases to pursue when once he has begun, no matter what hinderances he may meet on the way.

According to **Samuel Wilson,**

"I have concluded after my research that people with strong dedication can do anything and everything in life. No one can stop them from succeeding. They are ready to risk themselves for their aim and nothing is impossible for them."

The clearer you are about what you want and what you willing to do to get it, the more likely it is that you will be lucky and get what you want. Clarity of desired goals is a magnet that draws good luck to you. Goals give a direction to the enthusiasm and they point out to the end results. The world stands aside to let anyone pass who knows where he or she is heading towards.

Light a fire within yourself. Get motivated and excited about your mission. Become a ball of fire. Every day repeat the mission of your life hundred times till it enters every cell of your body, till every drop of your blood plays the melody of your mission. You have to drink your mission, eat your mission, sleep your mission, breathe your mission and live your mission.

Lord Edward George Bulwer-Lytton said:

"The man who succeeds above his fellows is the one who early in life clearly discerns his object, and towards that object habitually directs his powers."

Life must always have some purpose, a noble and worthy one that may lift life intellectually and spiritually. One such purpose, most relevant during student life, is the acquisition of knowledge. Knowledge dispels darkness and lights up uncharted vistas of progress. Knowledge generates self-confidence in a student, which will also make him intellectually adventurous and enterprising.

Norman Vincent Peale provides us the way to success—

"Have a clear goal, not a fuzzy one. Sharpen the goal until it becomes specific and clearly defined in your conscious mind. Hold it there until, by the process of spiritual and intellectual osmosis, it seeps into your unconscious. Then you will have it because it has you. Surround this goal constantly with positive thoughts and faith. Give it positive follow-through. That is the way success is achieved."

When you look for something you will find it. If you constantly expect exceptional success, you will surely have it. Peak performers attract success. You must keep the goals you desire to achieve at the forefront of your mind throughout the day. Repeat your ambitions at least five times a day, and visualise yourself achieving them.

**

14

Control Your Mind Through Meditation

Our mind is a source of tremendous power. If you can concentrate this power of mind at one place or at one activity, it will work wonders and you will accomplish wonderful things. But the tragedy is that it is very difficult to concentrate our mind on a particular point. The result is that all the powers and energies of mind get dissipated in various directions and the effect is not powerful. The rays of the sun cannot burn a piece of paper, but if the rays of the sun are concentrated or focused on the piece of paper by using a lens, it will immediately burn the paper to ashes. In the same way the mind cannot perform wonderful acts if its power is dissipated in various directions, but if it is concentrated or focused on any particular act it will do miracles.

According to **Dr. Franz Alexander**,

"Mind rules the body – is the most fundamental fact which we know about the process of life."

The power that the unconscious mind can provide is beyond limit. We all know individuals who, in crisis, were able to perform incredible feats of strength or endurance. It is the unconscious mind that produces for poets, prophets, scientists – indeed all creative thinkers – their deepest insights.

According to **Oliver Wendell Holmes**,

"What lies behind us and what lies before us are tiny matters compared to what lies within us."

Swami Vivekananda has rightly pointed out that knowledge is inherent in man. No knowledge comes from outside. All comes from inside. We say Newton discovered gravitation. Was it sitting anywhere in a corner waiting for him? It was there in his own mind; the time came and he found it out. All knowledge that the world has ever received comes from the mind; the infinite library of the universe is in your mind.

We should not try to control someone else. It won't work. Think about a newborn infant – how much control do you have over whether it wants to play, eat or cry? And you think you can control an adult? Control yourself first and then only you will be truly ready to exert a positive influence on others.

Once during his wandering days, swami Vivekananda was sharing a railway compartment with two Englishmen, who on seeing his dress took him for an illiterate beggar and began to ridicule him in English. At the next station they were astonished to hear him talking with the stationmaster in perfect English. The two Englishmen were ashamed. They asked him why he had not protested against their silly jokes. With a smile, Swami Vivekananda replied, "Friends, this is not the first time that I have seen fools."

Swami Vivekananda had great mastery over mind. He could control his mind as he liked. It is significant to know that Swamiji remained calm even when provoked by those fools.

Epictetus rightly said,

"We ought to be more concerned about removing wrong thoughts from the mind than about tumours and abscesses from the body."

The mind is very restless. It is very difficult to control and rein such restless mind. Well it has been compared to the maddened monkey. There was a monkey, restless by its own nature, as all monkeys are. As if this were not enough, someone made him drink wine, so that he became more restless. Then a scorpion stung him. When a man is stung by a scorpion he jumps about for whole day; so the poor monkey found his condition worse than ever. To complete his misery a demon entered into him. What language can describe the uncontrollable restlessness of the monkey?

The human mind is like that monkey, incessantly active by its own nature; then it becomes drunk with the wine of desire, thus increasing its turbulence. After desire takes possession, comes the sting of the scorpion of jealousy at the success of others, and last of all the demon of pride enters the mind making it think itself of all importance. How hard to control such a mind?

Meditation is the process by which mind can be controlled to a reasonable extent. Meditation is the gate that opens infinite joy to us. Meditation is the power which enables us to resist our slavery to nature. Nature may call us, "Look, there is a beautiful thing!" I do not look. Now she says, "There is a beautiful smell; smell it!" I say to my nose, "Do not smell it" and the nose does not smell it. In meditation you can change this slavery to nature. This is the power of meditation.

The mind can cause or cure disease. Cheerfulness, tranquility, courage, self-confidence, determination – such positive states of mind are more efficacious than any tonic in keeping the body healthy. It is the mind that shapes the body according to its requirement, like silkworm weaving its own cocoon. Wise men say that, it is the mind that liberates man or enslaves him.

According to **C.W Wendte, "Success in life is a matter not so much of talent and opportunity as of concentration and perseverance."**

People normally use only 8-10 percent of their total brain power. If we are able to concentrate our mind in the proper way we can start using the remaining 90 percent also. Concentration enables you to look directly at the heart of your problem so that you can decide the exact steps to take to overcome it. Very few of us have any idea of the immense power of our mind. Seldom do we use our mind effectively to get what we want. More often than not, we use it to get exactly the opposite – what we don't want! Poison or ambrosia can be produced with the material called 'thought'. If we understand the nature of mind, the way in which the mind functions, and able to control its functioning, we can produce ambrosia instead of poison.

Meditation should be practised twice every day and the best times for meditation are towards early morning and early evening, which are the two periods of calmness. Your body will have a like tendency to become calm at those times.

Our sense organs are totally governed by the mind. So if we are able to take care of our mind our sense organs are automatically taken care of. Mind is the only cause of man's bondage or freedom. Mind tamed and trained, is one's best friend; but unrestrained, it is one's worst enemy. If the mind is engrossed in sensual pleasures, it results in bondage; if it does not meekly surrender to them, the result is salvation. So, control the mind and sense organs will produce celestial music capable of transporting us to divine ecstasy.

All our actions and accomplishments are the outcome of our emotions, thoughts and imaginations. If we feed healthy and noble thoughts and emotions into our mind, then we can reap happiness, peace and contentment. To make the nature's computer called 'mind' more useful it must be fed with impartial observation, unselfish attitude, concentrated effort and a sense of humour. But it becomes useless if it is fed with inertia, carelessness, and lack of concentration, anger and pre-conceived ideas. Therefore, one has to be careful about what one feeds into this mind.

Swami Vivekananda gives a method of meditation. He says, **"Think of a space in your heart, and in the midst of that space think that a flame is burning. Think of that flame as your own soul and inside the flame is another effulgent light, and that is the soul of your soul, God. Meditate upon that in the heart."**

You must keep the mind fixed on one object, like an unbroken stream of oil. The ordinary man's mind is scattered on different objects, and at the time of meditation too, the mind is at first apt to wander. But whatever desire arises in the mind, you must sit calmly and watch what sort of ideas are coming. By continuing to watch in that way, the mind becomes calm.

Do not spend your energy in talking: meditate in silence. Do not let the rush of the outside world disturb you. When your mind is in the highest state, you are unconscious of it. Accumulate power in silence and attain bliss and calmness.

Somewhere I had read the following beautiful lines—

Be careful of your thoughts
For your thoughts become your words
Be careful of your words
For your words become your actions
Be careful of your actions
For your actions become your habits
Be careful of your habits
For your habits become your character
Be careful of your character
For your character becomes your destiny.

Walter Dill Scott said:

"It is more than probable that the average individual without any injury to health, can increase his efficiency by 50%."

I have a friend who has devised a little trick of auto-suggestion that works wonders for him. Whenever he is working on any assignment he listens to the rhythm of his own breathing, then would imagine that with every exhalation he is breathing out negative ideas and with every inhalation he is breathing in positive ones. With every exhalation he would say to himself, "I am breathing out failure" and with every inhalation he would say to himself, "I am breathing in success."

Norman Vincent Peale says:

"Nurture negative thoughts over a long period of time and you are going to get negative results. Your subconscious is very accommodating. It will send up to you exactly what you send down to it. Keep on sending it fear and self-inadequate thoughts and that is what it will feed back to you. Take charge of your mind and begin to fill it with healthy, positive, and courageous thoughts."

It has been rightly said by **Guru Nanak**—

"He who conquers his mind, conquers the world."

A person can learn to control his mind through prayer, company of good men, regular study of elevating and sacred books and by inculcating food habits. If one follows these instructions with patience, perseverance and sincerity, one is sure to succeed. It is wrong to say that we are too busy for prayer, when we are never too busy for meals and rest.

Swami Ram Tirtha said:

"Ships when they keep sailing in the sea for a long time, become a little deranged, are put out of order. They require to be placed in the dock for some time to be repaired. Similarly by keeping yourself too long in worldly affairs, in worldly matters, in the midst of spoiling and wearing and tearing surroundings, you are put out of order. You get your inner natural powers of inspiration lost. Just as you keep with your ships so should you do with your bodies? Keep your bodies, for sometime at least in the docks, away from those influences. Read books which will inspire you, live in the company of people who will inspire you, live alone by yourself. Devote some time to meditation and you will regain your power of inspiration."

If you can control your mind, all your emotions will be under control. For example, like anger, if not controlled, can create havoc in your life. Anger is temporary madness. Any decision taken in the state of anger will always be a wrong decision for which we have to regret later on. So never take any decision until your anger cools down. Remember that the creator has placed a marvellous reservoir of courage, energy and wisdom that we seldom use. This reservoir is the subconscious or, more exactly the unconscious mind. Like a dynamo it furnishes the power and drive of our lives. This power takes many forms. What we call intuition, for example, is nothing but a "still, small voice from the unconscious".

⁂

15

Power of Patience and Perseverance

I commence this chapter with the beautiful words of **Henry David Thoreau**—

"I know of no more encouraging fact than the unquestionable ability of man to elevate his life by conscious endeavour."

I know a student named Nilanjan Palodhi who is a living example of what one can do and achieve with perseverance. Nilanjan sat for West Bengal Judicial Service after his graduation in law. In his first attempt he cleared the written exam but could not clear the viva-voce. He did not lose hope and prepared for once more and this time he cleared the written as well as the viva–voce and secured his name in the merit list. But unfortunately all the vacancies were not filled up and since his name was at the lower end of the list he could not make it. It was a case of 'so close yet so far'. Any other person would have become depressed and would have lost hope and become frustrated, but not Nilanjan. He believed in the power of perseverance and patience. He had faith in himself. He believed in the philosophy that "effort never goes in vain". He believed in the divine law. He believed in the divine justice. He once again started preparing for the judicial exam. This time he cleared the written, viva-voce and secured his name at the upper end of the merit list. He is now a Judicial Magistrate posted somewhere in West Bengal.

Nilanjan had come to meet me after his selection in the judiciary. I had told him, "Your name will find a mention in my book and your name and achievement will inspire so many people to move patiently towards their goal and never to become frustrated."

According to **Henry W. Longfellow,**

"The heights great men reached and kept were not attained by sudden flight, but they, while their companions slept, were toiling upwards in the night."

Before we think in terms of success, we should put into action all our faculties and should be committed to the struggle. With this kind of attitude, success will follow, but even if it does not, since we have enjoyed the struggle itself, we shall not end up in being frustrated. No struggle ever goes waste. One unrewarded struggle will make us more determined and since we will also have learnt through experience, our renewed efforts will surely be crowned with success.

Let me tell you an inspiring story as was told by **Sadhu Vaswani**.

Tetsujen was a deeply devoted and committed Buddhist monk. It was his dearest wish to undertake the monumental task of translating and publishing the great Buddhist scriptures into the Japanese language. He was convinced that this was the only way by which the Buddhist religion could reach the masses. He knew that the project would entail great expenditure. But with undaunted spirit, he set up a public fund and zealously began to collect the money required. At the end of ten long years, when he had enough money to start his task, a terrible flood ravaged the district where he lived. Spontaneously, Tetsujen gave away the entire fund to be spent in the service of the victims of the flood.

However, he was not going to abandon his original mission. He started afresh with his collections which again took another ten years. This time too, another calamity struck the people, and Tetsujen gave away his huge collection to help the victims. But Tetsujen was one of those rare people who never, never gave up. He started a collection for the third time and took more than a decade to reach his target.

Now at long last, the Buddhist scriptures were available to the Japanese people in their own language, thanks to the perseverance and 'never say die' attitude of Tetsujen.

Thomas Alva Edison said:

"Seventy-five percent of world's failures would not have failed at all, if they had only kept at what they were trying to do."

A Japanese proverb says – "Fall seven times, stand up eight". This proverb was fully implemented in his life by **Abraham Lincoln**. Here is an interesting fact from his life—

He failed in his business in 1831.
He failed in his first step at politics when he was defeated for the Legislature in 1832.
His sweetheart died in 1835.
He had a nervous breakdown in 1840.
He was defeated for the elector in 1840.
He was defeated in his first attempt to be nominated for the congress in 1843.
He was defeated in his aspirations to be the Commissioner of the General land office.
He was defeated for the congress in 1848.
He was defeated in the Senatorial election in 1854.
He was defeated in his attempt to become the Vice-president in 1856.
He was again defeated in the Senatorial election in 1858.
He was elected the president of United States of America in 1860.

A stone cutter never feels defeated. He keeps on hammering. Maybe the rock does not split or crack even after 50th hammering. But it is quite possible that that it might break at 51st hammering. So the point here is that it is not the 51st hammering alone which split the stone but it was the combined effect of all the previous hammerings which caused the stone to break into pieces. Thus if the stone cutter would have left the job after 50th hammering, saying "It is impossible to break the stone and I had enough", he would have returned as failure but just see how close he was to success, just one hammering away!

For every achievement there are hurdles, there are hindrances – which you need to strike away, with a positive attitude. Kites rise not with but against the wind. For great achievement, the greater the difficulties you have to face, the greater the glory you will be bestowed upon.

John Ruskin said:

"The highest reward for man's toil is not what he gets for it, but what he becomes by it."

Look at the perseverance of a honeybee. It makes more than 4000 trips from flower to flower to collect one single tablespoon of honey. Edison succeeded in making the electric bulb after 10,000 failed attempts. N.R Narayana Murthy, along with his friends, started Infosys with a very small capital. They had to strive hard for years but later it grew to be a great company.

People who become great are those people who persist, people who persevere in spite of all the obstacles and hardships. Never stop running. Work hard, keep patience and never give up. Efforts never go in vain. In short run the fruits of the efforts may not be visible but in long run it is bound to bear fruits. This is the divine law and I assure you it is hundred percent true.

Every morning in Africa, a gazelle wakes up. It knows that it must run faster than the fastest lion, or it will be killed. Every morning, a lion wakes up. It knows that it must outrun the slowest gazelle, or it will starve to death. It doesn't matter whether you are a lion or a gazelle, when the sun comes up, you must be on a run.

I am sure you may have read this following poem many times but still I want you to read it one more time. It will inspire you and charge you. I try to read this poem as many times as possible in a day. The poem goes like this—

When things go wrong, as they sometimes will,
When the road your are trudging seems all uphill,
When the funds are low and the debts are high,
And you want to smile, but you have to sigh,
When care is pressing you down a bit,
Rest, you must – but don't you quit,
Life is queer with its twists and turns,

As everyone of us sometimes learns, and many a failure turns about,
When he might have won had he stuck it out.
Don't give up, though the pace seems slow,
You might succeed with another blow,
Success is failure turned inside out, the silver tint of the clouds of doubt,
And you never can tell how close you are, it may be near when just seems so far,
So stick to the fight when your are hardest hit,
It's when things seem worst, that you must not quit.

I had read a very inspiring story in 'The Complete Works of Swami Vivekananda' which goes as follows:

There was a great sage called Narada. Narada was a good yogi and very great. He travelled everywhere. One day he was passing through a forest, and saw a man who had been meditating until the white ants had built a huge mound round his body – so long had he been in that position. He said to Narada, "Where are you going?" Narada replied, "I am going to heaven." Then the man said, "Ask God when he will be merciful to me; when I shall attain freedom." Further on Narada saw another man. He was jumping about, singing, dancing and said, "O Narada where are you going?" His voice and gestures were wild. Narada said, "I am going to heaven." "Then ask when I shall be free," the man said. Narada went on.

In the course of time he came again by the same road and saw the man who had been meditating with the ant-hill round him. He said, "O Narada did you ask the Lord about me? What did he say?" Narada said, "Lord told me that you would attain freedom in four more births." Then the man began to weep and wail and said, "I have been meditating until an ant-hill has grown around me and I have four more births yet!"

Narada went to the other man. "Did you ask my question?" Narad said, "Oh Yes. Do you see this tamarind tree? I have to tell you that as many leaves as there are on that tree, so many times you shall be born, and then you shall attain freedom." The man began to dance with joy and said, "I shall have freedom after such short time."

A voice came, "My child, you will have freedom this minute." That was the reward for his patience and perseverance. He was ready to work through all those births, nothing discouraged him.

Never consider defeat and remove from your vocabulary such words as 'quit', 'cannot', 'unable', 'impossible', 'failure', 'unworkable', and 'hopeless', for they are words of cowards and fools. Remember winner never quit and quitters never win.

According to **Swami Vivekananda,**

"Never mind the failures, these little backslidings. Make attempts thousand times and if you fail thousand times, make the attempt once more. Take your time and you will achieve your goal."

Remember it takes a child nine months to grow in the womb of its mother and only then it becomes ready to come out of mother's body. Just think what would be the consequence, if the mother loses patience and says just after three months to take the child out.

After coming out of mother's body the child grows in size gradually. The growth is not perceptible in one day. After two of three months the growth becomes perceptible. It means that the child was growing in size everyday. Now if the parents of the child lose patience and try to increase the size of the child in one day by pulling his legs and head, you can well imagine the result of such an act.

So we find that nature itself teaches us to be patient and then only we can succeed in our mission.

We all can take lesson on perseverance from the life of the following personalities:

Michelangelo persevered for eight years to complete his painting, "The last judgement". Noah Webster was able to compile his dictionary after thirty-six years of perseverance. Leonardo da Vinci persevered for ten years in perfecting his painting, "The last supper". Milton persevered every morning from 4 p.m. to write "Paradise Lost". Ernest Hemingway reviewed the manuscript of his book "The old man and the sea" eighty times to bring perfection in his work.

According to **Charles R. Swindoll,**

"Great accomplishments are often attempted but occasionally reached. What is interesting and encouraging is that those who reach them are usually those who missed many times before."

Never live in hope and expectation with your arms folded. You can never have something without doing something. You will succeed when you pay the price for success.

Johann Wolfgang Von Goethe said:

"The important thing in life is to have great aim, and to possess the aptitude and the perseverance to attain it."

Success did not come easily for the great scientist Albert Einstein. As a young man he had considerable difficulty getting a job, and this became especially vexing after his father died and he needed to support his mother. One is reminded of Swami Vivekananda's plight after the death of his father, when it seemed no one was willing to hire him. None of Einstein's difficulties ever soured him on humanity.

Arnold fox says:

"If you have difficulty staying the course, take it a step at a time. Do what needs to be done today. Do not worry about tomorrow or next month. Persevere one day at a time. Dare to go on! Repeat your affirmation for perseverance 20 times a day, all day long, to remind yourself that you are giving it ten thousand more tries, if that's what it takes, because you are not going to give in."

Every failure is a dress rehearsal for success. Every opportunity for success also contains the possibility for failure. Never, never, never quit or give up. With ordinary talent and extraordinary perseverance, all things are attainable.

⁂

16

Realise Your Divinity

We are an aspect of divine and the source of infinite strength and power is open to us in God-realisation. We celebrate each birthday, each new year with such great fanfare as if it were a landmark event in our life. What would be our reaction if we paused to ask ourselves, "What have we done with our life during the year that has just gone? Have we moved closer to our goal? Have we moved closer to God?"

Depend on the fine thread of truth, the fine thread of reality. If you feel your divinity, if you realise your divinity it does not matters where you live, in the deep forests or in the crowded streets, that realising of Truth will convert everything, will change the whole world.

Thieves break into a house only when it is unguarded. If the house is kept lighted all the time, they dare not steal into it. Keep in your mind the light of Truth ever ablaze, no devil of fear or temptation will approach you. Believe in the Law Divine. Timid prudence makes a downright atheist of you.

Dr. Earl L. Diuglass says,

"Happiness is the gift of God. The reason so many people fail to find happiness is that they do not know where to look for it. They think they will find it in wealth; but money alone never made anyone happy. They think they will find it in ease; but freedom from responsibility produces restlessness more often than it produces happiness. They seek after social position, thrilling types of pleasure, places of honour; and often they try to find happiness in some gross indulgence.

They are on the wrong road. So long as they live they will never find happiness along any of these highways; and that for the simple reason that happiness is in our hearts, or it is nowhere. It is condition of inner life not of the outer. Its chief characteristic is peace, not possession; contentment not ambition; love and sacrifice, not pleasure and indulgence. It comes when a man stops fighting the universe and rests himself in the hand of the One who has made the universe and still manages it – when he stops trying to find happiness in the world and looks for it in his own heart."

In a forest full of thorns it is impossible to walk barefoot. One can do so if the whole forest is covered with leather, or if one's own feet are protected with leather shoes. It is not possible to cover the whole forest with leather, so it is wiser to protect one's feet with shoes. Similarly, in this world man is troubled with innumerable wants and desires, and there are only two possible ways of escape from them, viz., either to have all those wants satisfied, or give up all of them. But it is impossible to satisfy all human wants; for with every attempt to satisfy them, new wants arise. So it is wiser to decrease one's wants by contentment and the knowledge of your divinity and truth.

According to **Swami Vivekananda**,

"Every moment we are enjoying the Absolute Bliss, though covered up, misunderstood and caricatured. Wherever there is any blessing, blissfulness of joy, even the joy of the thief in stealing, it is that Absolute Bliss coming out; only it has become obscured, muddled up, as it were with all sorts of extraneous conditions and misunderstood."

Sadhu Vaswani tells us a story about a seeker who sat down to pray and meditates on the banks of the holy river Ganga. His aim was to find God and seek union with the divine. But the more he prayed, the farther he was from his goal. After several days of futile devotion, he arose from his meditation, crying our bitterly, "O Lord where are you? I seek you and find you not; my devotion has been in vain. I can only reach the sad conclusion that you do not exist."

At that moment, a fish jumped up from the river, crying, "Water, water, I have looked for water in vain. Where is the water? All my swimming and searching has been in vain. I die of thirst and I can only come to the sad conclusion that water does not exist."

"You are stupid indeed," scolded the seeker. "You are living in water, moving in water, breathing in water. There is water all around you. How can you die of thirst?"

"So is it with you, O seeker," said the fish. "You are of God. God is within you and outside of you. He is manifest in the whole wide world, and yet you say you cannot find Him. Open the eye of the spirit and behold him everywhere!"

So saying the fish leapt back into the water. It had taught the seeker a valuable lesson – God is everywhere. God is within you. All you need to do is purify your mind and heart in order to behold His beauteous vision.

We are ignorant of our true nature. We identify ourselves with the body, with the physical form, which is smaller than a speck of dust in the infinite vastness of the cosmos. We identify ourselves with our profession and social status, which is about as insignificant as a grain of sand on your table.

Iron appears red-hot in the furnace, but becomes black soon after it is taken out. In the same way worldly men are full of religious emotions as long as they are in a temple, in the society of the pious; but sooner do they leave these associations, than the flood of devotion in them subsides and again they forget their divine nature.

A spring cushion is pressed down when one sits upon it but soon resumes its shape when the pressure is removed. So it is with most of us. We are full of religious noble, high and spiritual sentiments as long as we hear religious talk; but as soon as we enter upon the routine of our daily life we forget all those high and noble thoughts and become as impure as before.

B Jivan Yati Maharaj once told an interesting story about French Pilot Ronald Nikson. French Pilot Ronald Nikson was flying his plane and he and his four colleagues were trying to locate the defence facilities of the German army during World War I. They entered German air space and were hiding their plane behind clouds. Nikson needed to clearly view the defence sites, so he took the risk of lowering his plane. His plane was hit. The German army was firing at them and the plane was in flames.

Nikson later wrote of the incident: "I was a non-believer in God. Observing that my burning plane was losing height rapidly and would soon crash with no chance of survival, I murmured, 'If there is God, save me'. I went blank after that. On regaining consciousness, I was told that I remained unconscious for almost two months. When I inquired about my colleagues, I was told that somehow the burning plane re-entered French border territory and fell there. Nothing remained, none of the others survived – except the Pilot.

After getting discharged I started going to church and inquiring about God from various priests. If God exists then I should find him and talk to him. I was not satisfied with the answers I got and eventually began reading many holy books. My desire to meet God increased day by day. After all he was my saviour. I was advised to visit India to learn further about God. I was informed that sages of ancient India had researched deeply into this topic. I resigned from the Royal Air Force, and came to India in search of God."

Nikson came to India and took up a position as professor in the English department at Lucknow University. Nikson familiarised himself with the Indian scriptures including the Gita, the Upanishads, the Vedas and the Srimad Bhagvatam. He took the name of Sri Krishna Prema. He established a centre at Mirtola in Uttar Pradesh now known as 'Uttar Vrindavan'. It is said that he realised the Supreme Lord here and used to talk to the Lord.

Let us also realise the Supreme Lord who always resides in our heart. Let us not be like the parrot which repeats the name of the Lord the livelong day but forgets the name of the Lord and cries in its natural way when caught by a cat. We may perform many pious and charitable acts in hope of earthly rewards but at the approach of misfortune, sorrow and poverty we forsake piety and charity.

Water poured into an empty vessel makes a bubbling noise, but when the vessel is full, no sound is heard. Similarly, the man who has not realised his divinity and the almighty is full of vain disputation about his existence and nature. But he who has realised his divinity enjoys the divine bliss. Most of us talk 'bagfuls' of religion and noble things but do not practice even a grain of it. The wise man speaks little, even though his whole life is religion expressed in action.

A newcomer to a city should first secure a comfortable room for his rest at night, and after keeping his luggage there, he may freely go about the city for sightseeing. Otherwise he may have to suffer much in the darkness of night to get a place for rest. Similarly, after realising one's divinity and after securing his eternal resting place in God, a newcomer to this world can fearlessly move about doing his daily work. Otherwise, when the dark and dreadful night of death comes over him, he will have to encounter great difficulties and sufferings.

Swami Jagadatmananda's following words are bound to make us pensive:

"Man observes people dying around him, relatives leaving the earthly abode, and is surprised. For a moment he feels sad. Then he may perhaps console himself by telling, 'Everyone has to die, sooner or later.' But he often refrains from asking the question, 'What is death? What is beyond death?' Of course he is shocked when close relatives expire. He feels intense agony of the parting caused by death, feels helpless, dejected and profusely sheds tears. But after a few days, gradually he overcomes the grief. He gets immersed in the daily routine of life. When death approaches him, he dies unprepared, in utter agony, pain and fear."

Only a man who has understood the true nature of death and his divinity can remain serene and courageous in such circumstances. Therefore I say, realise your divinity by constant prayer and by moving on the path of righteousness.

There are pearls in the deep sea, but you must hazard all perils to get them. If you fail to get at them by a single dive, do not conclude that the sea is without them. Dive again and again and you are sure to be rewarded in the end. So also in the quest for realising your divinity and the Lord. If your first attempt to realise your divinity and see Him proves fruitless, do not lose heart. Persevere in the attempt and you are sure to realise Him at last.

**

17

We Need Man-Making Education

Modern education teaches us how to make a living but it does not teach us how to live. It teaches us how to learn a few formulae and equations and get good marks but it does not teach us how to solve the problems of life. It does not teach teenagers how to control and focus their mind and increase the power of concentration. It does not teach us how to develop positive attitude in life which is very important to deal with various problems of life.

Dr. S. Radhakrishnan said:

"Any satisfactory system of education should aim at a balanced growth of the individual and insist on both knowledge and wisdom. It should not only train the intellect but bring grace into the heart of man. Wisdom is more easily gained through study of literature, philosophy and religion. If we do not have a general philosophy or attitude of life, our minds will be confused, and we will suffer from greed, anxiety and defection. Mental slums are more dangerous to mankind than material slums."

A few days back I asked a group of first year law students what they want to become in life. Some of them said that they wanted to become judge. When I asked them the reason for their choice, they said that they wanted to become judge because a judge gets a handsome salary, a car, a bungalow and other allowances and perks. This is the level to which education has reached today. We are teaching students to become a judge not for giving justice but for making him eligible for leading a luxurious life.

Some days back one of my students who had cleared the UGC–NET examination necessary for lectureship came to me and said, "Sir, many junior students are asking me the secret of clearing the NET examination. They are asking me the method of studying for the NET examination. Now the question is should I divulge the secrets to them? If I divulge the secrets, then they will also clear it and thus there will be more competition for me in the teaching profession."

I patiently listened to him and then replied: "Knowledge is one of those possessions which increase on being shared with others. Imparting knowledge to others broadens one's own intellectual horizons and ennobles and enlarges one's vision of life. So parting with one's knowledge is the surest way of enriching one's own treasure. If we are in a position to spread knowledge, in particular, we should consider ourselves to be among the most fortunate. Moreover, since you are now going to join teaching profession you must always be ready to share your knowledge to guide and help others."

Mahatma Gandhi has said:

"That education is of value which draws out the faculties of a student so as to enable him or her solve correctly the problems of life in every department."

From one lighted candle or lamp, you can light many more candles and lamps. So is the case with education. One educated person can impart education to hundreds and thousands of others without any loss to his own self. In fact, sharing knowledge with others is bound to increase one's own knowledge.

Jean Piaget's comments on education are worth noting:

"The principle of education is to create men who are capable of doing new things, not simply repeating what generations have done – men, who are creative, inventive and discoverers."

We seek education and knowledge in order to make our life meaningful through selfless service of others. In case we forget this we shall have to acknowledge regretfully that our life has been wasted. Man was not made just to eat, drink and be merry. That is the level at which animals exist and man has to rise far higher in order to justify his being a man.

Education today has become mugging up certain information and vomiting it on the answer script and getting good grades and getting a job for earning bread and butter. We have forgotten that to learn to love, to learn to be honest, to learn to be kind, to learn to forgive, to learn to be grateful, to learn to be polite, to learn to be selfless is a part of education. Man-making education will remove corruption from the society and we all know that in a corrupt system the influential gets bail and the rest gets jail. Man-making education will produce honest judges. Just like a tree is judged by the fruit it bears, a judge is judged by the kind of rulings he delivers. One cannot expect fox to be the judge at the trial of geese.

When students are sent into various educational institutions to get education, they are also expected to grow into young men and women of good moral character. And one of the cardinal principles of character is to be unselfish, or not being greedy. Greed is responsible for most of the evils rampant in our society. It is the bane of modern life. Our greed is a symptom of our neglect of spiritual values. The desire to get more marks than we deserve and the use of unfair means for this purpose is also a kind of greed. Mother Earth has adequate stocks to feed all the mouths, but there is not enough to quench the greed of even one person. If we could curb our grabbing tendencies and learn to live by accommodating the needs of one and all, there would be harmony and prosperity for each one of us.

Listen to what the famous American psychiatrist **Henry C. Link** has to say on modern education:

"That in personality traits, people with practically no education equal college graduates; that the people who have

the highest scholastic intelligence are just as likely as not to be lowest; those who are lowest in intelligence tests are just as likely as not to rank highest; that although the personality of some students improves during the high school and college ages, that of others deteriorates, so that the net result is zero. In other words there is no average improvement of personality due to education."

Dr. Link further says:

"The more intellectual the man, the wider his range of ideas, the more danger he is in putting the gods of temporary expedience before the god of everlasting values."

Both human and animal instincts co-exist in human psyche. It is difficult to predict when an evil instinct may raise its ugly head in our heart. So, we have to be on guard against them all the time and our education must help us in this matter. If they are not overcome at the very outset, they may strike roots and then it may be impossible to eradicate them. Our well-known saying "Nip the evil in the bud" has a great deal of practical wisdom.

According to **Barendra Kumar**,

"Education does not end with textbooks, rather it starts with them. Reading dozens of books on environment, on pollution, but never bothering to plant a seedling in lifetime – can this be termed as education? Storing hundreds of scientific laws but never wondering to make use of it for human need – can it be called education? Enjoying all the national holidays in the name of our national heroes, but never aspiring to spend some moments on reading, learning, knowing them, their efforts – is it real education?"

A student should bring passion to his study of a subject. Knowledge should be an obsession with him. In this world where people often get obsessed with unworthy and trivial things, there is nothing deplorable about being obsessed with knowledge.

Mahatma Devesh Bhikshu said:

"People have wasted lives in reading books to acquire knowledge, but mere reading of books does not make anyone learned. A truly learned person is he who understands the value of love in life."

If you pile all the books of Central Library on a donkey it will not make it learned and educated. You have to assimilate the knowledge to become learned If the poor and downtrodden stink in your nostrils, I can bet that you have still not become learned.

A man woke up at midnight and desired to smoke. Therefore he wanted some fire, for which he went to a neighbour's house and knocked at the door. Someone opened the door and asked him what he wanted. The man said,"I wish to smoke. Can you give me a little fire?" The neighbour replied, "Well, what is the matter with you? You have taken so much trouble to come and awaken us at this hour, while in your own hand you have a lighted lantern!" What man wants is already within him but due to ignorance he still wanders here and there searching for it. True education removes this ignorance and brings out the hidden gems in the person.

True education consists in the simultaneous and balanced development of the intellectual and spiritual faculties of a person. It is man-making education alone that imparts knowledge and learning to a person and enables him to discharge his duties efficiently and effectively thereby making his own life qualitatively better and making this world a more congenial place to live in. If you hand medical books and a stethoscope to a child, it does not amount to education. Do not expect that by doing this he will become a doctor.

A person does not need just information to get educated because education is not just a degree. Education is training in excellence from childhood onwards, which makes a man passionately desire to be a perfect citizen. Education is that which grants you freedom. It makes you self-reliant and self-sufficient. If even after being educated you are dependent on someone else for the fulfilment of your needs, it means that the process of your education has been lacking in something essential.

Man-making education will make us better human beings and consequently better father, better husband and better brothers. Shiv Khera has rightly said that the incidents of rape and molestations in the society are like a slap to those brothers who get Rakhi tied on their wrist with the commitment to protect their sisters. It is a slap to those husbands who take the oath at the time of marriage that they would protect their wives. It is a slap to those cowards who do not have the guts to protect the dignity of womenfolk in a cultured society. That education is of value which draws out the faculties of a student so as to enable him or her solve correctly the problems of life in every department.

According to **Martin Luther King Jr.**,

"The prosperity of a country depends not in the abundance of its revenues, not in the strength of its fortifications, nor in the beauty of its public buildings, but it consists in the number of its cultivated citizens, in its men of education, enlightenment and character."

Man-making education is that education which liberates you, which grants you freedom. It makes you self-sufficient. Our education must teach us to remain steadfast on the path of truth in face of all adversities. Truth is the basis of a noble character and we must protect the character whether wealth comes or goes. If required we should be prepared even to go through the 'test of fire' in order to safeguard the truth, bearing in mind that we shall emerge from this test purified and strengthened. Mud bricks are always in danger of disintegrating and giving way when subject to heavy rains but not the fire-baked bricks. Having once been through fire, they are strong enough to face rain or storm.

In the days prior to independence, enlightened, educated men occupying eminent positions in society were filled with high patriotism and were ready to face the bullets of the British and shed their own blood to liberate their country. Many of them lost everything and spent their days in jail. The ideals of service and sacrifice, which they had accepted as a way of life, were soon forgotten by the latter-day politicians and leaders.

Chakravarthi Rajagopalachari predicted what the situation could be if these high ideals were given up. He said:

"As soon as we attain independence, elections and what they produce corruption, the arrogance of officials, the inefficiency of administration, all will render the life of people a hell. People will regretfully remember the rule, which they had witnessed earlier, just, efficient, honest and peaceful. The only consolation is that we have been free from indignity and slavery. We can hope for a better life only through a liberal universal education. Only through such education citizens can imbibe right from childhood values like good conduct, faith in God, love and peace. In its absence there will be wide spread injustice and squandering of money."

Charles H. Spurgeon said:

"Education is a companion no misfortune can decrease, no crime can destroy, no enemy can take away. At home a friend, abroad an introduction, in solitude a solace, in society an ornament. It chastens vice, guides virtue and gives grace to genius. Education may cost financial sacrifice but in both money and life values, it will repay every cost hundredfold. The doorstep to the temple of wisdom is the knowledge of our own ignorance."

Einstein was also a great believer of education that wasn't regimented, one that gave students the freedom to pursue their interests and figure things out for themselves. He said: "Education should train students to think, not cram their minds with facts." The principle of education is to create men who are capable of doing new things, not simply repeating what generations have done. Man-making education makes the man competent to differentiate between right and wrong.

Swami Vivekananda says:

"The education which does not help the common mass of people to equip themselves for the struggle for life, which does not bring out strength of character, a spirit of philanthropy, and the courage of a lion – is it worth the name?"

People have wasted lives in reading books to acquire knowledge, but mere reading of books does not make anyone learned. A truly learned person is he who understands the value of love in life. In addition to providing enlightenment, an important purpose of education is to enable students to overcome negative tendencies like cruelty and replace them by positive, constructive tendencies like love. If education does not kindle love and fellow-feeling in a person, his education has been a futile process. Education does not consist in mechanical assembling of facts in one's mind. It is a process of self-purification and upliftment.

⁂

Epilogue

Dear readers, now that you have finished reading this book the first thing which you might have realised is that, there is no artificiality about this book. Everything is practical and related closely to our lives. The facts mentioned in this book are time-tested and they have been found to be true. I myself have tested and experimented with the facts mentioned in the book and found that they are true. The truths mentioned in this book have changed my life in a positive way and I am sure that same will happen with your lives.

I hope readers will be able to connect themselves with the book and find the tips and information given in the book useful. I am sure this book will go a long way in improving your personalities, your lives; make you a better person and help you in reaching your goals in life.

As is the case with all the self-improvement and personality building books, this book should be read more than once. Rather you should go through each chapter many times so that the thoughts mentioned in these chapters are properly assimilated. The stories mentioned in the book are very inspiring and they can be told to the children and younger generation to mould their lives in a positive way and build their personalities.

I assure you readers that this book will solve most of your day-to-day problems. You will find solutions to most of your problems in the chapters of this book. This book will act as a guide throughout your lives and if it is so, I shall consider that my purpose of writing this book has been fulfilled.

Remember progress in life is like climbing up a steep hill. As you ascend higher, the hill starts getting narrower, till when you reach the top, there is room only for one person. If you want to be that one person, you will have to be the best. Work hard to reach your goal and the pinnacle of glory and then work hard to retain it. You may fall a million times. Never mind. Get up and walk again.

I would like to mention a few lines from my 'Baba's teachings—

Life is a song – sing it
Life is a game – play it
Life is a challenge – meet it
Life is a dream – realise it
Life is a sacrifice – offer it

Let us all once again pay heed to the roaring voice of **Swami Vivekananda: "Arise, awake and stop not till the goal is reached."** Death is at the doorstep and there is so much to do and achieve. Do not sleep any more. Do not waste your time anymore. Just start marching towards your goals and STOP NOT TILL THE GOAL IS REACHED.

**